To the Islands

Kerry Howe spent a career writing internationally acclaimed books about Pacific/Polynesian/New Zealand history. Now an Emeritus Professor, meandering in a 50-year-old wooden yacht, he reflects on his lifelong engagement with the Hauraki Gulf islands.

CW01639456

Also by Kerry Howe

(Editor), *Vaka Moana. Voyages of the Ancestors. The Discovery and Settlement of the Pacific*

Coastal Sea Kayaking in New Zealand

The Quest for Origins. Who First Discovered and Settled New Zealand and the Pacific Islands

Nature, Culture and History. The 'Knowing' of Oceania

(Editor, with Robert Kiste, Brij Lal), *Tides of History. The Pacific Islands in the Twentieth Century*

Singer in a Songless Land. A Life of Edward Tregear, 1846-1931

(Editor), *The Verse of Edward Tregear*

Where the Waves Fall. A New South Sea Islands History From First Settlement to Colonial Rule

Race Relations Australia and New Zealand. A Comparative Survey 1770s-1970s

The Loyalty Islands. A History of Culture Contacts 1840-1900

To the Islands

Exploring, remembering, imagining the Hauraki Gulf

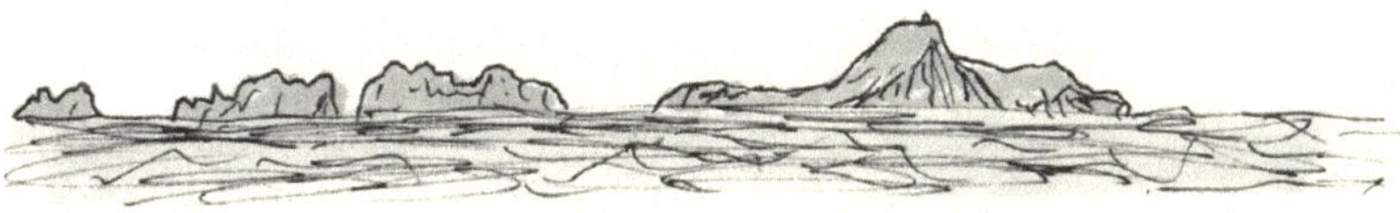

Keith & Eda

Kerry Howe

read all about some decent sailing areas

best wishes Kerry

MOKOHINAU ISLANDS PRESS

Published by
Mokohinau Islands Press
49 Settlers Grove
Orewa
Auckland 0931
mokohinauislandspress@gmail.com

First published 2016

Copyright © Kerry Howe, 2016

The right of Kerry Howe to be regarded as the author of this work in terms of the Copyright Act 1994 is hereby asserted.

All rights reserved. This book is copyright. Apart from fair dealing for the purpose of private study, research, criticism or review, permitted under the Copyright Act, no part may be reproduced by any process without the prior written permission of the publisher.

978-0-473-35203-5
Typeset and designed by Smartwork Creative, www.smartworkcreative.co.nz
Illustrations by the author
Edited by Geoff Walker
Printed by Yourbooks.co.nz

Front cover photograph: Mercury at Moturekareka
Back cover photograph: Grey Group and Broken Islands from Kaikoura Island

for Paul Lauren

scholar, fisherman, amicus

Contents

Maps

Preface

Over a third of all New Zealanders live within sight of the islands of the Hauraki Gulf. Most are familiar with the characteristic outlines of Rangitoto, Browns Island/Motukorea and other nearby islands, as well as with the lofty peaks of distant Great Barrier/Aotea and Little Barrier/Hauturu Islands. Aucklanders think highly of the Gulf and are proud of its attributes and recreational possibilities. They have embraced the Department of Conservation's branding of them as Treasure Islands. But probably relatively few citizens actually visit any Gulf islands, beyond perhaps Waiheke or Rangitoto, which are the only ones served by regular short ferry trips from the city.

Given the limitations of public transport, only the more adventurous with boats can truly explore the islands' features. Even so, the islands of the Hauraki Gulf are so numerous, scattered and diverse that it can take decades, perhaps a lifetime, to get to know them even reasonably well, and every visit to the same island is different due to seasons and weather. Furthermore, experiencing them 'now' is only part of their being, since over time, indeed since first Polynesian settlement and especially since European colonisation, they have undergone profound changes culturally, economically and environmentally. This book seeks to reveal some of the layers of change and continuity over time and to celebrate the wonders of the islands, while at the same time drawing attention to past, present and future challenges to the Hauraki Gulf's well-being.

Shirley Maddock's *Islands of the Gulf* and the TV series it spawned was an inspirational introduction to the islands for my generation. It is rightly regarded as a classic. But it was published 50 years ago. On rereading it recently I was suddenly struck by how much the islands have changed, and, more significantly, by how much we have all changed and how we view the Gulf so differently now.

As befits the modern age we have a range of new values and concerns, barely acknowledged in the 1960s, relating to environmental protection and conservation of the islands, of their native species and of their surrounding seas. Also thanks to modern scholarship and political shifts we now have a major interest in Maori culture and history, and over the last few decades we have seen complex efforts through Treaty of Waitangi processes to try to right some of the harsh legacies of colonialism. So it is time to update the record of place and how it is viewed.

Unlike some previous books on the Gulf that offer excellent fishing, cruising and tourist guides (such as those by William Owen, and Linda Bercusson and John Walsby), this book ranges more widely to try to capture the diversity and complexity of the region's nature, culture, history and politics. There is no existing single source that gives such a comprehensive cover of Gulf issues. To the general reader I make accessible research findings from a very wide range of subjects.

A glance at the large number of short chapters might suggest a random arrangement of places and topics, and in some cases it is; thus to some extent the book can be read randomly (maybe a chapter or two a night before falling asleep in a boat cabin) as a kind of Hauraki Gulf companion or notebook.

But there is also an underlying organisation tracing some basic and interrelated themes:

- an autobiographical thread which ranges from my parents' Gulf-related wartime activities to my lifelong fascination with the Gulf and my exploration of it.
- a recreational boating, especially sailing, theme. It is not a technical guide as such, but touches upon a myriad of maritime matters and the joys of sailing. My maritime adventuring is fairly gentle, more messing about in boats than daring feats before the mast.

- a chronological Maori history theme, ranging from first settlement, occupation and use, from traditional times to the musket wars, to early European contact issues, land alienation and recent actions through the Waitangi Tribunal and related processes of restitution.
- a chronological colonial-to-modern history theme tracing the economic/physical exploitation of the islands through to modern attempts at island restoration and wildlife preservation.
- a theme tracing prehistoric to modern environmental issues.

Anthropologists might describe my approach as that of 'thick description'; social scientists might talk of it as a 'cultural ecology'; post-modernists might mutter about it being 'self-reflexive'. It may be all these things, but, more simply, I'm inclined to regard my narrative as a personal and many-layered encounter with the Hauraki Gulf islands. It is essentially a lifelong love story about a place.

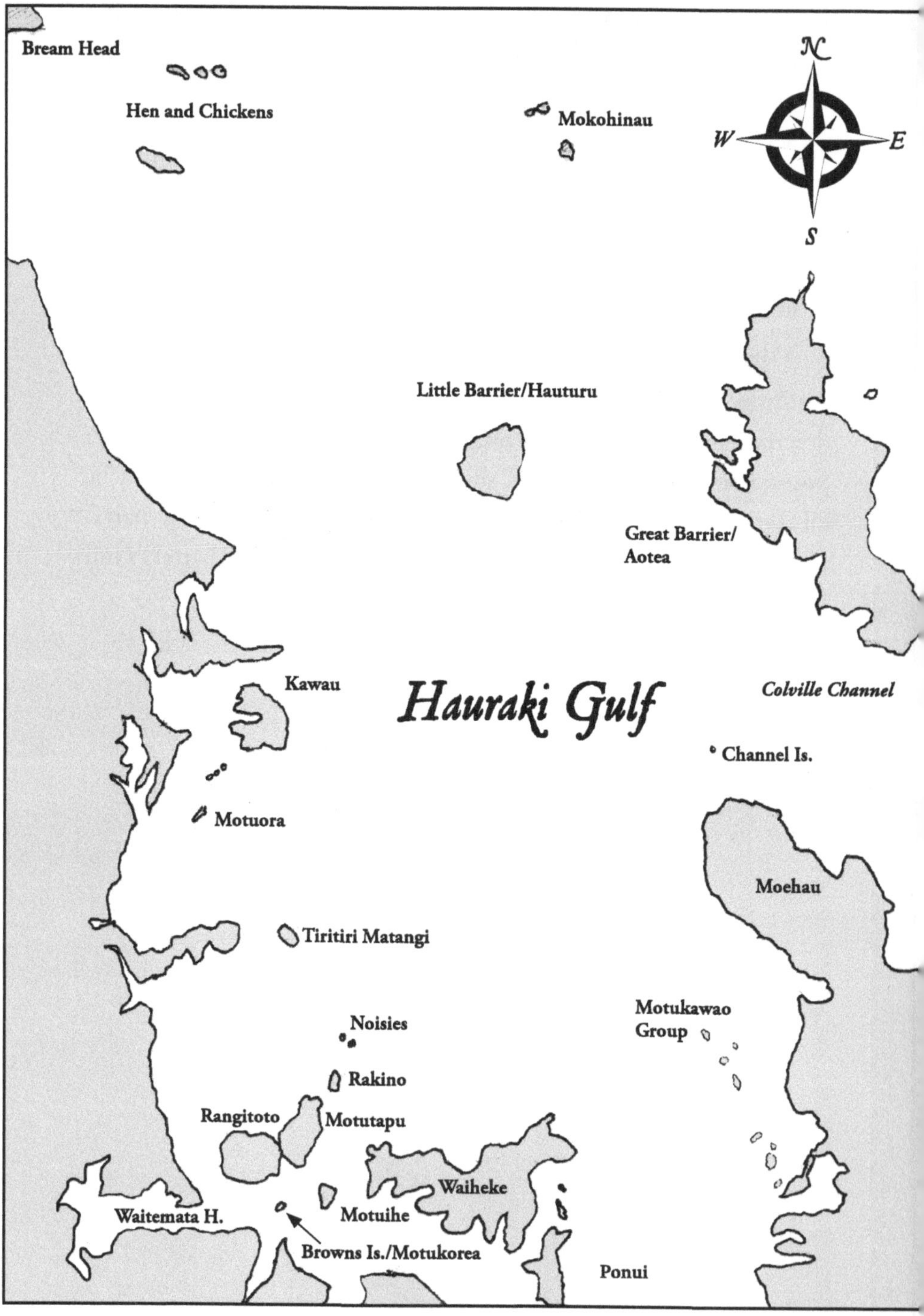
Bream Head
Hen and Chickens
Mokohinau
N
W
E
S
Little Barrier/Hauturu
Great Barrier/
Aotea
Kawau
Hauraki Gulf
Colville Channel
Channel Is.
Motuora
Moehau
Tiritiri Matangi
Motukawao
Group
Noisies
Rakino
Rangitoto
Motutapu
Waiheke
Waitemata H.
Motuihe
Browns Is./Motukorea
Ponui

Endings and beginnings - Narrow Neck beach

Among my earliest memories is the long profile of Rangitoto Island, summer-red pohutukawa trees and flashing navigation lights at night in the Rangitoto channel. I grew up in a post-war state house near Narrow Neck beach in Auckland.

Our primary school classes from Vauxhall School were sometimes marched down to the beach. A teacher would pace out a distance along the shoreline and plant a flag. We would try and swim to it. I remember perfecting, as it seemed to me, a swimming style which was a disguised way of walking along the bottom. For many years I was too skinny to swim properly. I just kept sinking.

The endless summers of youth, complete with sheets of peeling skin, were spent at the beach, fossicking on the rocks at either end, snorkelling in the murky water, sailing model boats, mucking about and learning to sail in a friend's tiny Sabot sailing boat. I desperately wanted a Sabot. At one stage my dad offered to build one for me, but I knew that it cost a great deal of money and my parents were quite poor so I declined, I hope gratefully. He was probably very relieved and never asked again.

But he did go out and buy an ancient kauri clinker dinghy that was wallowing around in Ngataringa Bay mud. Against all expert advice he glued marine ply strips over the dodgy bottom planks with a new, untested product called epoxy resin. That dinghy lasted for decades.

Then he got an old Johnson outboard propeller shaft and welded it to an Iron Horse two-stroke motor mower engine. It was the first air-cooled outboard, complete with retractable starter cord, on the harbour. If anyone had an outboard, which was not common in those days, it was usually a Seagull. He and mum often went out to the Rangitoto channel to fish. I loathed the two-stroke stench, and usually got seasick. Dad liked to anchor right in the shipping channel and we had a few scares when big ships came close.

But I loved playing in the heavy old dinghy, and with friends I would row for miles, including to Rangitoto to have adventures around the lava islets near the lighthouse. I did a lot of rock and dinghy fishing with my mates. I don't remember ever having life jackets, or my parents being the least concerned. We had full, free and safe range on bikes and boats.

Awareness of the sea beyond Narrow Neck came slowly. One boy at school, Jimmy Dixon, had a dad who skippered the gut boat – a dreadful old motorised barge that collected rubbish off the ships in the Auckland port and then allegedly dumped it in the sea on the other side of Rangitoto. The other side of Rangitoto became for me a place I wanted to go.

A local family, well above my family's station in life, owned a keeler. Every summer they loaded it up from a dinghy off Narrow Neck beach before sailing away somewhere, for weeks. I watched as blankets and pillows and boxes of food were loaded aboard. As a child the thought of sailing away and not coming back before dark was utterly thrilling. I ached to sleep on a boat, on the other side of Rangitoto.

Another boy in my Vauxhall school class, Robbie Woollacott, sometimes used to take me to his house at lunchtime at the bottom of the school grounds to watch his father (John) building a keeler in his front yard. Woollacott yachts have a proud heritage. I guess yachts were always somewhere in my psyche.

I had an uncle who had once been in the merchant marine, sailing to the islands of the Pacific on the Union Steamship boats. He told wondrous but outrageous sea stories. One of the best was about boiling up whole pumpkins in barrels at the stern of the ship and throwing them into the sea. The sharks that always followed swooped in, swallowing them whole. When their stomach juices worked through the seawater-cooled pumpkin skin the boiling contents were released, sending the sharks into paroxysms of leaping agony.

My all-time favourite book was/is a Giant Golden Book called *Pirates, Ships and Sailors*. My imagination in my younger days was a riot of ships and seas and islands. It still is.

But as a teenager, I turned my back on my Narrow Neck playground and instead went on surfing forays far from Auckland. Then came university and marriage and postgraduate study in Australia and the Pacific islands, and travel around the world, and then a family and a career as a university historian. For 40 years I studied and wrote about Pacific islands – their first settlement, their traditional cultures and histories, and how they responded to western contact. For many years I was based in one of New Zealand's few landlocked cities – Palmerston North. Though I wrote numerous books about the Pacific, and often travelled to the Pacific islands, that oceanic focus could never quite compensate for living so far from the sea.

So I took up river kayaking, when time allowed, which gave me access to water – of a kind. But rivers scare me, especially the bigger ones such as the Tongariro and Rangitikei. Their hidden snags and sudden swirls and upwellings seem so random. Taniwha perhaps. Sea conditions are far more understandable, even if at times just as difficult.

I started taking my river kayak to the coasts, around Kapiti and Mana Islands. Then I blew the budget completely and bought a proper sea kayak. Marlborough Sounds soon became a marvellous new playground. Queen Charlotte Sound was a favourite place, and D'Urville Island.

But there were always annual holidays, taking the children to old haunts in Auckland and Northland. Watching our children play each summer as I did on Narrow Neck beach was a special experience.

Eventually we returned to Auckland to live, now child free, and I spent another 10 or so years in academia. All the islands of the inner

Hauraki Gulf I explored by sea kayak with a vengeance whenever I could. I also ventured further afield, paddling solo from East Cape to North Cape, including to and around Great Barrier Island, over several summers.

I was a passionate sea kayaker, and wrote a book about the joys of coastal sea kayaking,[1] but always, deep down, I hankered for a real boat, one with sails, one with a bed and a cooker.

So later in life Merrilyn and I bought a 7.3 metre Alan Wright Pacer from an old sea dog in Thames. Our first 'official' sail when back in Auckland was to Narrow Neck beach. There was a steep learning curve, complete with Coastguard educational courses. We now own a 1966 Des Townson-designed and built 9.3 metre ('30 foot') kauri yacht in which we sail way beyond the far side of Rangitoto, exploring the whole of the Hauraki Gulf and further north. And we don't come back before dark.

My dad died relatively young, in his 60s, probably due to his experiences as a prisoner of war in Europe. My mum died aged 96. Their ashes are scattered off Narrow Neck beach.

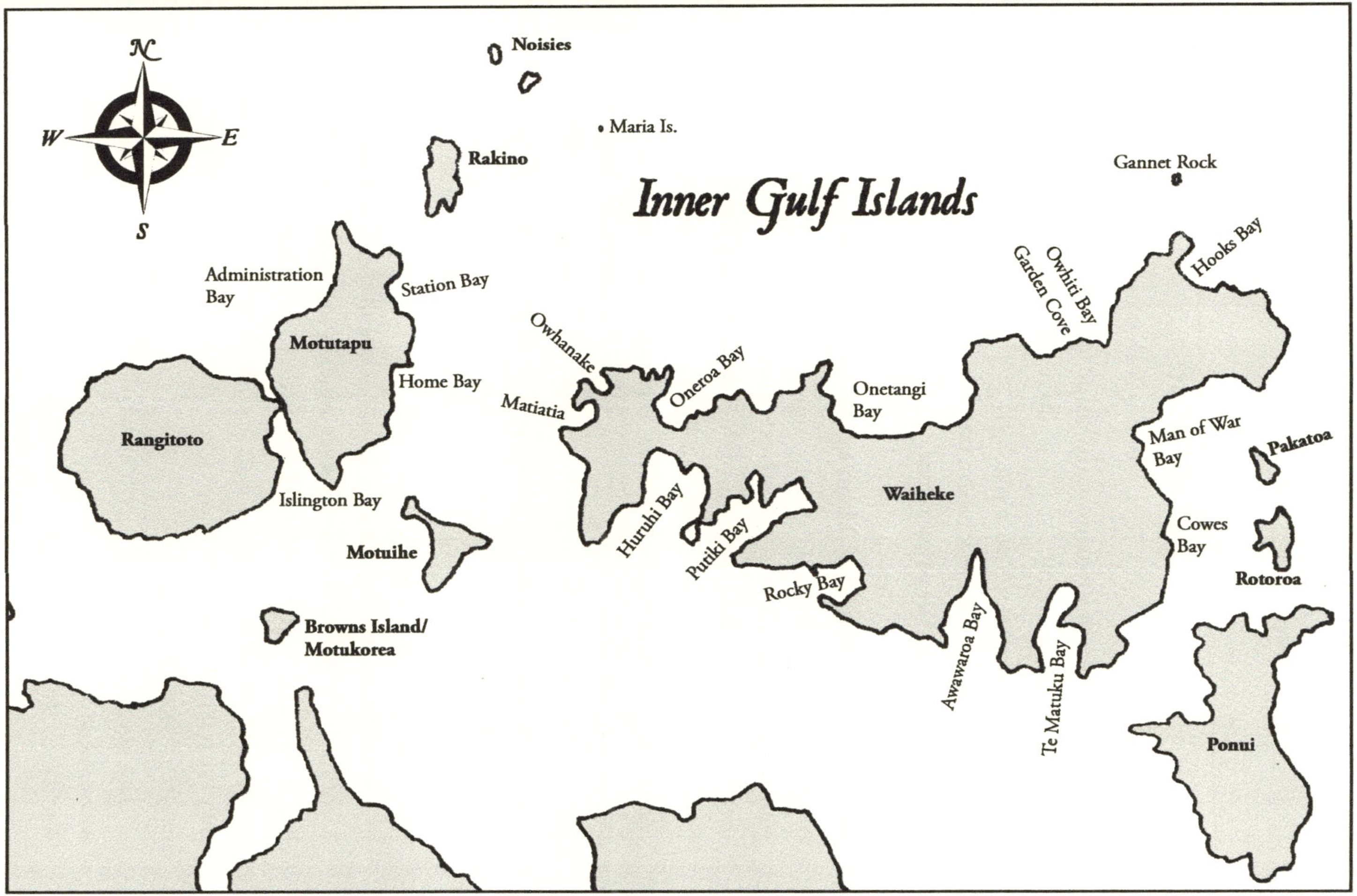

Inner Gulf Islands
N
W
E
S
Noisies
Maria Is.
Rakino
Gannet Rock
Administration Bay
Station Bay
Motutapu
Home Bay
Rangitoto
Islington Bay
Motuihe
Browns Island/ Motukorea
Owhanake
Matiatia
Oneroa Bay
Onetangi Bay
Garden Cove
Owhiti Bay
Hooks Bay
Man of War Bay
Pakatoa
Waiheke
Huruhi Bay
Putiki Bay
Rocky Bay
Awawaroa Bay
Te Matuku Bay
Cowes Bay
Rotoroa
Ponui

Rangitoto

It is always there, on the horizon. Its shape looks the same wherever you are around Auckland. And it is always a dull green-grey, even on the brightest day. When I was little you could see vast areas of bare lava from Narrow Neck beach, but over the decades they became increasingly covered in pohutukawa.

It came up out of the sea about 1400AD, the last piece (so far) of New Zealand to be formed. Maori were already here and watched the massive lava upwelling, and the boiling, steaming sea from nearby Motutapu Island where they had extensive gardens. Hundreds of their footprints, along with those of the Polynesian dog they brought from the tropics, are to be found in Rangitoto's thick ash layers on Motutapu. Latest research shows that there were two close eruption events. The first led to the emergence of the smaller cone which is now to the north of the summit. The larger summit cone and the smaller one to the south were built up in an eruption up to 20 years after the first.

The name Rangitoto may derive from the red spurting lava, or from the blood of Tamatekapua, chief of the *Arawa* canoe, when he was wounded in a fight with Hoturoa, chief of the *Tainui* canoe. Maori did not live on Rangitoto since water is too scarce and it was hardly the landscape for cultivation, but they would have made frequent visits to harvest seabird eggs and the birds themselves. And they are reputed to have deposited some of their dead there and some mauri, or sacred objects.

The colonial government purchased the island in 1854, and it was used as a source of basalt and scoria for construction work in Auckland city through to the 1930s. Much of this was taken from the area in Islington Bay, where a munitions base was later located during WWII. There was also a short-lived salt works established near Mackenzie Bay in the 1890s. A windmill pumped saltwater into pools that subsequently drained back through the porous rock leaving salt. The windmill blew down in the first storm. Many of the island's roads and the neat little roadside curbings and walls were built by prison labour during the Great Depression.

Also during the Depression over 100 small baches were built for recreational purposes around the shoreline, on a lease arrangement. No more were built after 1937. Most were removed by the 1980s, but a dozen or so still remain, some still under lease, some derelict, some renovated for holiday hire. I would love to stay in one. They are now regarded as historically valuable, showing how simple family baches used to be – no running water, no electricity, no flush toilets – before people started building utterly extravagant mega-size holiday homes elsewhere.

My first landing on Rangitoto was from our dinghy that my friends and I rowed from Narrow Neck beach. To this day I am enchanted by the rugged lava islets near the lighthouse. We played explorers and pirates. Then came family trips on the ferry boat with cousins. We climbed the rough lava track to the summit, and swam in the tidal pool on our return to the wharf.

But I never really got to know the island until my sea-kayaking days. We did dozens of circumnavigations. The highlight was paddling through the narrow passage that separates Motutapu from Rangitoto, right alongside some of the old baches and passable only at high tide. I always think of the irascible Samuel Marsden in 1820 ordering his small vessel to sail through the gap, then somewhat wider though not much deeper. He ran aground and had to be towed off by local Maori, doubtless laughing heartily at the good Reverend's reckless navigation.

We also had very many illegal overnight camps in a hidden location – perhaps the only spot on the entire 100 per cent lava island where there was enough leaf mould to enable me to push in tent pegs. The island became a regular overnight refuge from city living, just over an hour's paddle from North Shore beaches. We'd paddle over on Friday afternoon, drag the kayaks out of sight, cook a meal and drink red wine while the sun set, wait until just before dark to erect the tents, and depart next morning before a ranger could appear. None ever did.

Night views from that spot are spectacular – the city lights and flashing shipping channel beacons. Sleep in a tiny tent is often broken by the diesel thud of large ships entering and leaving the channel. You can feel it through the ground.

My mother spent most of the war years in the army on Rangitoto and neighbouring Motutapu Island as a gunner, manning the large guns on Motutapu and acting as a spotter and plotter in the observation bunker on Rangitoto's summit. I still have her highly detailed gun-operation manual, which she copied by hand into a notebook. There are many war remnants on Rangitoto, especially at the munitions dump at Islington Bay. In summer it might have seemed an idyllic island life, though the constant fear of Japanese invasion and the worry about my dad as a German prisoner of war must have been debilitating.

In her old age we were able to get her back to the summit of Rangitoto when the Department of Conservation started to run a tractor and trailer unit up the road for tourists. She took it all in her stride, without showing any obvious emotion even when, on the crater-rim track, she came across and entered a derelict concrete structure which had been her sleeping quarters.

We sometimes visit Rangitoto in our yacht, for picnics at Whites Beach or to anchor in Mackenzie Bay by the lighthouse and walk the road to the summit. Islington Bay is the only reliable anchorage though it is often spoiled these days by the hundreds of boats that congregate there in summer.

In recent times the island seems more colourful. For the first time in my life I've seen masses of pohutukawa flower, thanks to the successful eradication of possums, wallabies, cats and other predators. And native land birds are gradually returning to the silent forest after many generations of absence.

Motuihe

The island that came to my childhood consciousness after Rangitoto was Motuihe. A girl in my class at primary school, Fay Sowerby, had a dad who owned a large commercial motor vessel, the MV *Florence M. Kennedy*. My class was privileged to have our annual school picnic on it, usually at Motuihe Island. Other classes just walked down to Narrow Neck or Cheltenham beaches where they ate their packed lunches. Unbeknown to either of us Merrilyn, my future wife, was probably in one of these unfortunate classes. Her dad was a soldier then living in the nearby Narrow Neck army camp, where she had been born.

Motuihe became a special place. Even today I thrill when I see the Norfolk pines. One uncle worked at the *Auckland Star* newspaper and all the extended family used to be taken on specially hired ferry boats for the annual *Star* office picnic on the island. There was a grass strip along the beach on the sheltered western side, which seemed enormous at the time, where there were running, three-legged, sack, wheel-barrow, and egg-and-spoon races. There were lolly scrambles, plus an endless free supply of small cardboard tubs of ice cream complete with wooden spoons that came out of huge green canvas sacks full of dry ice. A highlight at the end of the day was to see the remaining ice tipped into the sea, where it bubbled and smoked.

The old Motuihe sports field is still there (though there is now a new one on higher ground atop the isthmus). The original one has been severely eroded – or my memory of its vastness is badly distorted. The sandy beach still flanks one side. As children we referred to it as the girls' beach since it is usually calm and shallow. Across the narrow isthmus, through the Norfolk pines, is the boys' side – a much larger and more exposed beach. Depending on which direction the wind blows, boaties can find shelter on one side or the other. But on the girls' side the tide drains out very quickly as low tide approaches, leaving large areas dry. It is most entertaining to see day boat owners panic when they realise their boats are barely floating and to see their prodigious and ultimately futile efforts to drag them to deeper water. Old hands simply wait for the tide to come back in. The boys' side is not without minor problems for it can be a very rolly anchorage thanks to the wake of frequent fast ferries racing to nearby Waiheke.

The island has had a varied history. It was inhabited by Maori, who had extensive gardens. It was heavily cleared of bush. Te Arawa had a very early interest, though Ngāti Pāoa and Ngāi Tai claimed ownership at the time of colonial settlement. Motuihe derives from Te Motu-a-Ihenga, meaning Ihenga's Island – Ihenga was a crew member of the *Arawa* canoe. There are two pa sites, the best one on the point between Ocean Beach and Snapper Bay. There are very many kumara storage pits and middens scattered across the island. They are readily seen as you wander across the still-open grasslands. But one day it will mostly be native forest once more thanks to very extensive replanting by volunteers.

Motuihe was farmed in early colonial times and bought by the Crown in 1872 to use as a quarantine station during a smallpox scare, and then again during the 1918 influenza epidemic. It was the prison home, before he escaped, of Count Von Luckner during WWI. During the Depression the quarantine station was turned into a children's health camp. After WWII it became a major naval training station.

The Motuihe Trust, formed in 2000, together with volunteers and help from the Department of Conservation, has turned the island from its former rabbit and weed-infested state to a beautiful pest-free nature-reserve island devoted to native-bird species protection and human recreation. Being so close to Auckland it can get very crowded with pleasure craft and ferry day trippers on summer weekends. The island's closeness to Auckland is both a curse and a blessing.

In older age we have made a number of sea-kayak camping trips to the island, and once I got publically embroiled with the Department of Conservation when I published a newspaper article complaining about the lack of regular ferry access, primitive camping conditions, stinking toilets, lack of drinking water, and the run-down state of the graves on the headland of those who died during the 1918 influenza epidemic. Things improved after that. I even got roped into a working party to tidy up the graves. These days the camping is by far the best and closest to downtown Auckland you can ever get. And not many people know about it. Views of Auckland's lights at night are simply stunning.

Gulf formation

The Hauraki Gulf did not always look as it is today. New Zealand, like most places, has a tortuous geological history. Much of the Hauraki Gulf and many of its islands consist of ancient sedimentary rock types associated with Gondwanaland, with later and complex sedimentary overlays as sea levels rose and fell, and as the land was buckled by plate movement and rent by volcanic outbursts.

The clashing of the Indo-Australian and Pacific tectonic plates created the mountain chain stretching from Great Barrier, along Coromandel Peninsula and further south, with land to the west faulting and subsiding, ultimately forming the Firth of Thames and Hauraki Plains region.

Volcanic activity periodically burst through the sedimentary mountain ranges forming the volcanic peaks we see today from

Great Barrier and along the Coromandel Peninsula. Volcanic activity elsewhere created Little Barrier as well as Hen Island (but not the Chickens) and the peaks around Bream and Whangarei Heads. Their rugged, rearing volcanic cores that seem to tear at the very sky are geologically identical to the high island peaks of eastern Polynesia, such as the Marquesas and the Society Islands. Only the climate is a bit different.

Other, lower islands also have volcanic origins, such as Mokohinau and Browns Island; the youngest is Rangitoto. And of course the whole of the Auckland isthmus is studded with volcanic cones. Remnants of volcanic activity can still be found in a few hot-water locations – at Great Barrier Island, Waiwera, Miranda, Whitianga and Hot Water Beach on the Coromandel Peninsula, and Parakai in west Auckland.

There were also some instances of mineral formation, such as localised manganese and copper deposits on Kawau and Great Barrier Island, and extensive gold in the Coromandel/Thames area.

The region also experienced major, repeated changes in sea levels over its geological history. During the last Ice Age sea levels were far lower than they are today. The whole of the Hauraki Gulf south of a line from about Cape Rodney across to Great Barrier and the Coromandel was above sea level. You can see this ancient shoreline if you follow the 100-metre contour line on marine charts.

The Waikato River did not turn left north of Mercer and drain into the Tasman Sea as it does today. Instead it continued northwards across what is now the Hauraki Plains region and beyond to the distant shore line. Glistening silica sand was sometimes washed down the Waikato River from the central North Island volcanic plateau, which is why the long beaches of Pakiri and Mangawhai, north of Cape Rodney, are so dazzlingly white. It is criminal that these sands are being mined close offshore. They can never be replaced.

Buying the first yacht

Once we had made the decision to buy a yacht, there suddenly seemed a scarcity on the market. We hunted about for some months. We looked at a few trailer sailers but decided to go for something slightly bigger.

Eventually a suitable vessel appeared on Trade Me, a 7.3 metre Alan Wright Pacer. But it was at Thames. I phoned the owner, who seemed an old-fashioned, decent sort who promised to hold it until we had seen it. We made the trip from Auckland to find a remarkable old sea dog, Phil Smallfield. His tiny house on the Firth of Thames estuary was like something from a kid's story book, crammed with every sort of nautical knick knack imaginable, plus a lifetime of family memorabilia. The walls were festooned with pictures and objects, and from the ceiling hung model ships and plywood gannets whose wings flapped when you pulled their strings.

It was soon apparent that he was something of a legend in the Gulf and along the Northland coast, sailing the yacht solo on a single trip for about five months every year. He had undertaken some amazing small-boat voyages, going three times to the Three Kings Islands, 30 nautical miles beyond the top of mainland New Zealand. His last trip there, at the age of 80, was in the *Sea Waif*, that now sat sadly on a trailer in his back yard, unused for several years due to his aging body.

He told us the name came from a book written by popular Cornish novelist Silas Hocking in 1910 entitled *Sea Waif*. The pathos had made him cry when he was a child. He showed us his treasured copy of the book.

It soon became apparent that he would not sell his yacht to anybody unless he deemed them suitable owners. I saw a flash of disappointment when he learned that we had not had a yacht before. But on our side was the fact that he was terrified that some young yobs might buy it for a party boat complete with beer flags. We had never heard of beer flags. When in the future we saw beer flags on vessels in anchorages we knew to give them a very wide berth.

So we sat for hours listening to his wonderful tales and instructions and his sea lore generally. It was clearly not going to be a quick change of ownership since he insisted that it would take many hours for him to point out all the marvellous features of his boat, which he wanted to sell about as much as his right arm.

Eventually we did a deal in principle and returned to Thames the next week for the full instructions, and more anecdotes, and it was all very educative and emotional. We were approved. We became good friends. Money changed hands.

He moved the vessel to the local boatyard where he rigged it. I returned with a friend to apply antifoul, and after a couple of days of painting and further instruction there was a tearful (on both sides) handing over of the keys. We set sail for Milford Creek in Auckland, *Sea Waif's* new home.

Merrilyn and I enthusiastically sailed the Gulf in *Sea Waif* for several years, on a steep learning curve. The distinctive yellow vessel was often recognised as Phil's. When we decided to move to a bigger boat we agonised over telling Phil. In the event he didn't seem to mind at all. And he was delighted that we bought a Townson since Des Townson was a friend of his. We kept up an email correspondence with him for several years, and visited him couple of times before he died.

Some of his sayings still ring in my ears when I'm sailing: 'There are only three rules. Rule 1 – never overpower your yacht. Rule 2 is the same as Rule 1. Rule 3 is the same as Rule 2'.

Or: 'Always dress her properly.' He demanded the optimum sail configuration for his own sailing. *Sea Waif* came with three jibs, one of which could be fitted to an extending pole that he used as a bowsprit, turning it into a cruising chute, plus a spinnaker. We never used these sails (we were too scared), and only used one jib that Phil called a blade – 'It will be the only one you'll ever need,' he'd said, knowing we were rank beginners. He had a horror of the slightest flap in any sail. To this day I sense his disapproving presence when I'm struggling with a sail flapping and cracking like a whip.

Buying the second (and last) yacht

Sea Waif was the perfect learning yacht for us, easy to sail and maintain. But after a couple of years we decided to get something a bit bigger that would go better upwind into the characteristic Gulf chop, and also have full headroom. *Sea Waif* had a pop-up cabin top to give full headroom only when at anchor, but deep down I wanted a 'proper' yacht, and also a wooden yacht. The yachts in the Gulf anchorages that most caught my eye, I eventually discovered, were designed by legendary Des Townson. There was something about their graceful sheer lines, and sense of balance and proportion, and their elegant window arrangements.

We aspired to a Townson 32, and looked at several but they were showing their age, needed some work, and above all were well beyond our price range. Then we came across a 1966 Townson 30, called *Mercury.* It was older, had a dodgy motor but was half the price of a 32. It was not only designed but also built by Des Townson. Besides, it was owned by a well-known Auckland boat designer and surveyor, so I figured that he would not want to be embarrassed professionally by selling something if the bottom was about to fall off it. In any case, I now had a few more clues as to what to look for when buying a yacht, and more idea of what best suited our purposes.

So *Mercury* became the new obsession, and credit-card drainer. We had a new engine installed. We cleaned and painted the hull inside and out. Decks were stripped and sealed. All the aged plumbing and wiring was ripped out. All current-sucking incandescent lights inside and out were removed and replaced by LEDs. A whole lot of ancient non-working equipment was ditched. We installed a new VHF radio, GPS plotter and fuel tank. We had an early anchor-drag scare in Port FitzRoy during a gale, so came back and bought the best anchor we could buy – a Rocna. And so on, and on, and on …

The non-standard feature of the boat was a stainless steel wheel in the cockpit, built by a previous owner reputed to be an engineer. It is very neatly attached to what looks like a truck steering box with a direct drive down the rudder shaft. It was also fitted with an old belt-drive Autohelm 3000. We thought we'd give it a go and that we would probably pull it out and replace it with the original tiller that is still stowed on the boat. But in the event the wheel has proved very successful, and the old Autohelm still does the business, so the arrangement has stayed – for now.

After six years we've got the boat as good as it will ever be in our time. Not a professional restoration but the vessel is neat and trim and tidy and bone dry, and everything works and she's very sea worthy. She has become my adored possession. She is so finely and elegantly crafted. There's not a straight line, or a square area anywhere. Every surface, vertical or horizontal, is lovingly and subtly curved. The only flat bits are the cockpit and cabin soles (floors), galley surface and seating/sleeping spaces. And if any paint gets knocked off anywhere (heaven forbid) there's a golden glow of kauri. I look after her obsessively. She lives at Gulf Harbour marina.

Like *Sea Waif*, *Mercury* is also often recognised by older hands in anchorages, especially since it was a successful racer on the Waitemata Harbour in the later 1960s and 70s.

Phil would be pleased for us. And he would be delighted that we sail extensively along the Northland east coast in summer – as far north as Houhora, if not to the Three Kings.

Simple sailing

Having arrived at playing yachts after many years of extensive sea-kayak touring and coastal camping, we found that keeping things small, simple and uncluttered on a yacht came easily. We did not succumb to the temptation to load up the considerable extra internal space that came with *Mercury*.

Equipment on our Townson 30 is fairly spartan yet efficient and sufficient. There's a gimballed single-burner alcohol stove (Origo 1500), a couple of pots and a fry pan. There is no fridge, no microwave, no TV, no running hot water. We survive fine for weeks without fresh milk or ice-cold drinks. We catch a lot of fish, and I consume cockles, mussels and oysters. Cabbage, carrots, potatoes and onions usually last for ages. Packet food, especially with pasta and noodles that simply requires heating, is now good quality, and there is a wide variety of excellent canned food. Rice is always a basic standby. Bread can either be baked after the shop stuff goes off after a few days, or replaced by all sorts of rice and corn-based crackers. Good old cabin bread can sometimes be found in country shops. Red wine (requiring no cooling) will keep for ages if required, but seldom has much chance.

Even basic food takes on a taste of haute cuisine when spending time on the sea. One of the great joys of sailing is to be in a snug anchorage with a glass of wine and a simple meal, sitting in the cockpit watching the sun set.

I don't like supermarket shopping, but cruising through the supermarket shelves as the final act before a trip can have a certain attraction. I call it provedoring, a marvellous, antiquated term that makes me think of old marine things like Stockholm tar and brass oil lamps. As the items are loaded into the trolley they are envisaged in their future roles, being used or consumed in wonderful anchorages or on the move on the open sea.

We always have a fishing line out in anchorages in the hours before eating, just in case a nice snapper decides to provide us with a tasty meal. And one often does.

Our yacht has a 100-litre stainless-steel water tank. On longer trips we also have about another 100 litres of water squirrelled away in soft-drink bottles stuffed into every empty niche. It's good to be water independent for weeks at a time. There are relatively few places on Gulf islands where boats can take on reliably clean water.

Our auxiliary is a 20hp Beta motor. It's never missed a beat, touch wood. There's a toilet and holding tank. Bodies are kept clean with travel wipes, and rinsed after swimming with freshwater from soft drink bottles heated by the sun.

We run a simple rig – a large furling genoa and mainsail. No spinnaker or cruising chute. We don't do bad-weather sailing, or take risks. We don't sail through the night. We are not the fastest yacht in the bay. But maybe we sail about more often and probably a lot further than most.

First settlers

Europeans have been around in the Hauraki Gulf for some 200 years. Maori have been here for 700 years. First human settlement in New Zealand dates to about 1300, and some of the earliest arrivals were likely to have been in the Hauraki Gulf region. Maori were certainly present in some numbers and already leading a settled gardening and fishing life when Rangitoto erupted from the sea in the early 1400s. Evidence of human activity has been uncovered below its ash layer on neighbouring Motutapu Island.

Maori have a direct cultural and genetic ancestry to communities generally referred to as Austronesian in South-east Asia at least 6000 years ago. About 3500 to 4000 years ago some of these people began what was to become perhaps the greatest human migration. To that time, all of the earth's major continents had been settled by humans walking to them. But the myriad islands of the Pacific Ocean could never be reached on foot. Their human discovery and settlement had to wait until the development of an oceanic sailing technology and the capacity to transport, plant and harvest crops, for the pre-human Pacific islands were very poor in food plants.

It was the Austronesians who developed these skills. They ventured out on revolutionary outrigger voyaging canoes with sails, bringing with them over 30 plants, including coconut, yam, taro, banana, sugar cane, and their dogs, pigs and Asian jungle fowls together with various hangers-on like the Pacific rat (*Rattus exulans*) or kiore. By 3500 years ago they were travelling around New Guinea (where they picked up more plants such as kava and breadfruit) and down the Melanesian island chain, and 3000 years ago they reached Fiji, Tonga and Samoa. Then they made eastern Polynesia 1500-2000 years ago and radiated out from there. Some reached Hawaii, others Easter Island and South America (where they deposited some of their Asian jungle fowls, and returned to eastern Polynesia with the sweet potato).

In the final probe some travelled far to the south, probably from the southern Cook Islands, and reached New Zealand. This makes our country the last habitable place on earth to be settled by humans.

Of the animals they had when they started their journey from South East Asia, only the dog and the kiore reached our shores. Most of the tropical plants they might have brought here could not survive, though taro, yam, bottle gourd, paper mulberry and *ti* plant survived, although taro and yam struggled somewhat in New Zealand's colder climate. But perhaps critical to the successful colonisation of New Zealand was the sweet potato (kumara) that came from Chile and thrives in a temperate climate. Much of the New Zealand landscape, at least as far south as Christchurch which was the growing limit, still remains pock marked with tens of thousands of kumara storage pits.

I spent many years in my academic life studying the first human settlement and colonisation of the Pacific islands and writing learned tomes. These days, when sitting in some Gulf anchorage at sunset, I'm more content to muse more fancifully on the first Polynesian settlers making landfall, if not in the Gulf, then possibly nearby. Sooner or later, I think, they would have cruised by, perhaps in this exact spot. Just around the corner, at Tairua, the only artefact found so far known to have come from the tropical Pacific is a pearl shell fishing lure. There is no pearl shell in New Zealand.

The peoples of Polynesia were used to finding new lands, of course, but in so many ways New Zealand was so different, with its colder climate, its dense forests, its vast new array of land birds, notably the moa, and its seals which had colonies all around the New Zealand coast. What would they do first? What did they think? Were they cold and desperate? Did they foresee this as a new home? What were their priorities?

The actual moment of Polynesian arrival has always fascinated me. As a child I was once taken to the Auckland Art Gallery and saw Charles F. Goldie and Louis J. Steele's huge painting called the 'Arrival of the Maories in New Zealand' (1898) depicting an emaciated crew on a damaged double-hull canoe spotting land in the distance. The distraught sailors' red eyes and protruding ribs and their frantic pointing to the stormy shore left a deep impression.

Of course knowledge gained later in life sometimes has the capacity to ruin childhood thoughts. In this case Goldie and Steele's painting, I learned, was directly modelled on Théodore Géricault's painting of the 'Raft of the Medusa' that the pair had copied in their art studies in Paris. I have used Goldie and Steele's painting on the cover of one of my books about Pacific prehistory, *The Quest for Origins.*

For a while after Maori first got here, perhaps for a 100 or more years, some made the trip back to eastern Polynesia, via the Kermadecs and maybe even Norfolk Island, and others continued to arrive from Polynesia, but eventually the long two-way ocean voyaging died out. No one else arrived. New Zealand became a new and isolated world, the southern outpost of Polynesia. Social and economic adaptation was the key to successful colonisation both before and after European arrival.

First settlements

The tiny founding groups initially had plenty of resources – especially fish, shellfish, land birds, notably the various species of moa, myriad seabirds, and seals and sea lions. It was a hunting and scavenging lifestyle, although early on they also planted the kumara and learned the technique of storing the tubers over winter. They wrapped them in dry vegetation, packed them into bags, and stored them in pits under shelters for both eating and replanting in early spring. They were not like today's plump kumara, but were much smaller and often nobbly, and some were thin like fingers.

There were no moa on Hauraki Gulf islands, and seal colonies were mostly on the eastern side of the Coromandel peninsula, but generally Gulf island food gathering and growing was much the same as on the mainland. There is some discussion about how growing conditions may have been better on islands since they can have microclimates moderated by the sea and are thus slightly warmer on average than inland mainland places.

The favoured islands for settlement tended to be the larger and more fertile ones such as Waiheke, Motuihe, Motutapu and Great Barrier, as well as smaller ones close to the Auckland isthmus – Browns Island/ Motukorea and Rakino. But most other islands also show evidence of kumara planting, with some taro in swampy areas and gourds as well. Maori also learned to eat the beaten, boiled, glutinous roots of bracken fern that rapidly appeared after any bush firing and clearing.

All islands have some traces of human activity, either permanent or temporary. But by modern standards the populations were always relatively small. At the time of European contact there may have been as few as 100,000 Maori in the whole of New Zealand, so even the larger mainland individual settlements might number in the hundreds rather than thousands. Certainly the Auckland isthmus was a major centre of Maori populations given its very rich volcanic soils, harbours and rivers. All Gulf island populations were variously linked to their mainland tribal groups across the wider Auckland region. The estimated population of the region in about 1800 is some 6-7000.

In general, Maori settlement on islands was based on a mixed economy of shellfish gathering, fishing, birding and gardening, much as on the mainland. Some islands had more specific resources and uses, such as seabirds, shellfish, fish, obsidian (especially from Te Ahumata, Great Barrier), and the more commonly found argillite and basalt. They might also be useful as refuges, and/or defensive positions.

While the populations grew and there were occasional military and political upheavals, subsistence economic life in the Gulf seems to have remained relatively unchanged over many hundreds of years, until the arrival of the West.

In search of taro

Ancestral Polynesians brought over 30 tropical plants across the Pacific Ocean from South-east Asia and New Guinea. Most could not survive in New Zealand, but one that did was the taro plant, albeit as a fairly poor specimen with much smaller corms and far less food value than in the tropics, especially in tropical Polynesia where it became a major staple.

I have seen remnants of wild taro in some damp gullies in Northland but never in the Hauraki Gulf, though it has sometimes been reported in archaeological sites. Reading one archaeological report on Kawau I noticed that some taro was supposedly growing behind George Grey's house alongside the little creek draining into Ladys Bay, some up by the waste-water ponds, and some on the Redwood Track.

So one midwinter day I set sail for Kawau on a mission to find the taro plant. It was a fine day with not much wind, in contrast to the storm-force winds that had battered Auckland just two days before and had been recorded as peaking at over 100 knots at Tiritiri Matangi. The sea did not look rough though it was alive with residual energy, all peaky and bouncy, brown looking and full of seaweed. But it was also sparkly due to the sun's low path across the sky only a few weeks away from the shortest day. I anchored in Two House Bay, a favourite, and was the only boat in the Mansion House Bay area – the joys of winter sailing.

The late-afternoon skies darkened and ran started spitting as I started to walk up the Old Coach Road. Everywhere massive pine trees had been toppled and branches stripped in the recent storm. Looking out for taro's large leaves, very familiar to me from my Pacific island travels, all I could see were exotic Arum lily plants everywhere. I started through the darkening bush, off the track, around the waste-water ponds. No luck.

Wandering down the Redwood Track I began to lose heart. The only largish leaves were those annoying lily plants. I made several forays through the wet, tangled undergrowth, gave up, and returned to the track not far from the huge redwood tree. And there was a stand of taro, in the marshy growth, right beside the track. I'd walked this track dozens of times and never noticed them. You only see what you look for.

I took a few photographs using the flash and touched one of the big dripping leaves, far, far bigger than a lily leaf. So here it was with its genetic ancestry going back to South-east Asia, 4000 years ago, brought here by canoes across the world's largest ocean, at the extreme edge of its survivability, at the southernmost tip of Polynesia, growing wild in the wet, darkening bush.

Waiheke

I first heard of a place called Waiheke from my grandmother. Or more specifically I learned of a place called Cowes Bay. I imagined a bay full of cows. In the 1930s my grandparents, on my mother's side, would take their numerous children and camp at Cowes Bay for some six weeks each summer. It must have been pretty remote and isolated in those days, though old photographs show a long wharf (now long gone), and supply steam ferries periodically arrived for the farming families. My grandparents took all their gear and food for the duration, and lived very simply, cooking on open fires. The kids roamed about unsupervised all day. No mod cons, no endless child management and cosseting.

Waiheke is the largest of the inner Gulf islands. Its rolling hills and valleys were extensively settled and large areas cleared by Maori. Almost 800 archaeological sites have been identified, and settlement sites are readily visible. Waiheke was strategically significant to Maori, lying on the crossroads, or sea roads, of the Auckland isthmus and the Coromandel/Thames region and beyond. Which is why it was the most fortified of all the Hauraki Gulf islands with some 50 defended pa sites, and why its Maori history is a complex tale of competing interests and conflicts. Paul Monin, the island's historian, and indeed the only person to write a scholarly history of any of the Hauraki Gulf islands, sums up its pre-European history 'as a place passed constantly by travellers and periodically by conquerors ... It is not surprising that on the eve of first European contacts no tribe could claim through whakapapa exclusive rights.'[2]

Its name is variously interpreted – ebbing waters, descending waters, trickling waters. I rather like the one which says that it refers to the time that the *Arawa* chief's son peed on the shore.

If Maori appreciated the island's potential, so too did early colonial settlers. Stands of kauri were cut out, other timber was felled for firewood and building timber in Auckland, and there was some manganese mining. Right across the 19th century, land for sheep and cattle farming was inexorably transformed block by block to private European and government ownership, and by the early 20th century subdivision for residential sections was under way. This land alienation has left a legacy of injustice for Waiheke Maori that is only now being addressed through the Waitangi Tribunal. In 1989 the 800-hectare Waiheke Station at the eastern end of Waiheke was transferred by the government to Ngāti Pāoa. It is one of only two significant areas of land in Maori ownership in the Hauraki Gulf/Auckland region (the other is in Katherine Bay, Great Barrier Island).

In the 1950s one aunty and uncle were very friendly with a larger-than-life character called Bunty Brown who lived at Blackpool. They would make weekend visits to Bunty and his family on an old steam ferry, or the diesel-powered *Baroona,* sometimes taking me along. The steam ferry, which was probably the SS *Muritai* (or was it the older *SS Onewa*?) was a dreadful old thing, rolling and wallowing in the slightest sea. Passengers used to give a collective groan when they realised that they were in for a steam trip. Depending on the weather such a trip could take well over an hour, sometimes two in really bad seas. Waiheke was traditionally very poorly served by ferries until quite late in the 20th century.

In the evening Bunty would settle into a massive armchair, pour himself a copious glass of his home brew (my uncle did not drink, nor did the wives), and regale us all with amazing stories, none of which I remember now. But I do vividly remember watching his glass slowly empty, and the many refills. These were days when children were mostly to be seen and not heard, and I passively though pleasingly enjoyed the long evenings of tall stories. In pre-TV days adults often talked to each other, so there was a lot to listen to.

On a recent visit to Waiheke I tried to find Bunty's house, mainly by looking for a front yard with an open water course running through it and tangled macrocarpa trees, the only features of the property I remember. But the area is now quite gentrified.

Waiheke is a place of contradiction. Many of its western regions are quite spoiled by human settlement which sees shabby old baches – the more traditional Waiheke habitations – intermixed with ugly mega-architecture of the super-rich. Here too is the contrast of Waiheke as the permanent home for many modest, poor, and alternative-lifestyle people, and the largely temporary holiday home for the entrepreneurial wealthy.

The eastern region is mostly uninhabited private farmland, much of it owned by the Spencer family, equally exclusive and non-welcoming, but at least not being overrun, yet, by rampant 'development'.

In more recent times vineyards have appeared like mushrooms on the landscape. Fine vineyard wining and dining has become trendy. Add to this mix the mass summer influx of day visitors to beaches, cafes and vineyards.

Paul Monin's wonderful little book on Matiatia outlines the progress and perils of Waiheke's increasing popularity. He also provides the staggering information that Matiatia wharf, the main passenger entry for the island, had 1.6 million arrivals/departures in 2010, making it 'the country's second busiest passenger port' after those of the Cook Strait ferries.[3]

Waiheke, fortunately, is not typical of the Hauraki Gulf islands, most of which are now off limits to private housing, farming and commercial development.

Waiheke – sailing about

In my sea-kayaking days Waiheke was always a rather problematic place, since no legal camping was possible except at Rocky Bay. Thus a paddle from Auckland to the Coromandel or vice versa simply used this one stop as an overnighter on the way to somewhere else. The island was sadly never a destination in itself. The largest landowner, one of New Zealand's wealthiest families, the Spencers, reputedly had farm staff regularly check their glorious private coastline and beaches for illegal campers.

We finally got to know the island better when we started sailing our yacht. I love the small anchorage at Owhanake. It's exposed to the north-west, and even a strong south-westerly sends swells around into the bay and severe downdrafts from the surrounding hills. But the steep surrounds are striking. Going ashore there is a wonderful coastal walk to Matiatia in one direction, and a shorter coastal walk in the other.

Oneroa Bay is often very crowded and can be a rather rolly anchorage, but it does provide access to shops and cafes for those who need them. Onetangi has a superb long white beach and is much less commercialised. We thought we had found a perfect anchorage tucked inside Needle Rocks at Onetangi one day. But in the middle of the night a brisk south-easterly wind blew up and forced us to slog across the bay to the shelter of Piemelon Bay.

Tiny Garden Cove is impossibly beautiful. One week day we found it empty and chanced the extremely narrow entrance between rocks. I raced around the hills taking photographs of *Mercury* in the most beautiful, enclosed anchorage imaginable. But we had no intention of staying overnight. There would doubtless be other boats spoiling our solitude, and indeed as we left others did arrive, vying for very limited anchoring space.

Owhiti is the quintessential northern New Zealand beach, white sand, glowing pohutukawa in summer, hills and bush. But it will soon be spoiled by the inevitable luxury house stuck in it (as is also the case with neighbouring Cactus Bay).

Hooks Bay always has a certain drama to it, surrounded by high hills, opening out to a view of the Coromandel Peninsula. The water in the bay somehow always looks deep, though it's not, and the sea is always cold, probably due to the tidal currents whipping around Thumb Point. The now bare hillsides once sported major stands of kauri trees, soon toppled in the early colonial demand for the timber. There are some gouged kauri slides on the surrounding hillsides. Dotted across the pastoral landscape are numerous replanted stand-alone trees, each surrounded by a wire fence to prevent cattle browsing. Paul Monin has described how the unfortunate yet vividly coloured slips along the Hooks Bay coastline (and also at Owhanake) are the result of excavation of gravel and sand for the concrete-hungry building booms of early Auckland. If you know what to look for it is easy to read the landscape past and present while at anchor in Hooks Bay.

Man of War Bay, and its general area, is large and relatively sheltered and has lots of anchoring options, but can be fairly crowded. It takes its name from the numerous early British naval ships that took on water there before the fledging town of Auckland had proper provisioning facilities. The stream they used is readily found, though you would not want to drink from it now. This is the famed 'bottom end' of Waiheke and destination for so many recreational boats out of Auckland. In high season it can be a bit like dodgems. Mussel farms and a few reef dangers add to the sailing excitement. From its northern side you can climb a steep track through native bush and overlook Stony Batter and the whole of the Firth of Thames. Stony Batter features WWII tunnels and fortifications, as well as striking basaltic andesite rocks that cheekily poke out of the landscape, like so many tongues, or nipples.

Islands at the 'bottom end', notably Pakatoa and Rotoroa, have unusual histories. Pakatoa was the Salvation Army's drying out-refuge for female alcoholics from early in the 20th century until 1942. The island was sold in 1949 and in the 1960s it was destined to be a sophisticated recreational island resort, perhaps like Queensland's Hamilton Island, serviced by a futuristic hydrofoil, the *Manu Wai*. But the entrepreneur behind it all, Robert Kerridge of cinema chain wealth and fame, ran afoul of the seamen's unions over proposed manning levels, as did the next owner of the hydrofoil, the difficult Leo Dromgoole. The hydrofoil was laid up and eventually sold in Australia, and the project, which anticipated 20,000 visitors a year (which was considered a lot in those days) and service by two hydrofoil vessels, has never amounted to more than a collection of modest kiwi-style holiday chalets and a kind of conference centre. But better that than high rise. The island is privately owned and occasionally comes onto the market for eye-watering millions.

Neighbouring Rotoroa was the Salvation Army's alcohol treatment centre for males. It operated until 2005. In recent times it has been leased for 99 years to wealthy benefactors Neal and Annette Plowman, who have formed a trust, chopped down 20,000 exotic pines, replanted the island in 400,000 native trees, and removed predators. The Auckland Zoo has been engaged for a native bird, insect and reptile acclimatisation programme. There is also an attempt to start a gannet colony. The island is open to the public and features an excellent museum showing what life was like during the alcohol treatment days. There's a restored jail, schoolhouse and church to visit. There are walking tracks all over the island, and excellent beaches for swimming. In keeping with the tone of the island's past, there is still an alcohol ban ashore. Rotoroa is a fine example of how big money can be used for worthwhile purposes. No other island in the Gulf has been so rapidly turned from open farmland to a conservation masterpiece.

Waiheke's southern coastline is not usually considered a favoured boating destination because it does not have the fine sandy beaches of the northern side, some of its bays are fairly shallow and they are exposed to south-westerly winds. Yet because it is different it has great interest and some pleasing scenic features. There are long stretches of bushy coastline, and endless small stony coves ideal for picnics. Looking at a Google Earth image of Waiheke, it is interesting to note that most bush regrowth is generally right along the southern half of the island.

If there are northerly conditions, or if south-westerlies are light, the southern side of Waiheke is a great place for just messing about on a boat. And it's generally far less crowded in summer than the northern anchorages such as Oneroa, and at the 'bottom end'.

Best overnight anchorages on the south coast are in Huruhi, Putiki, Rocky and Awawaroa Bays. Rocky Bay, which has a potentially dangerous entrance and requires looking at a chart first, gives sea access to Whakanewha Regional Park. Te Matuku Bay is very shallow and thus has remained relatively undisturbed. It is now a valuable marine and scenic reserve.

Electronics

We live simply on our yacht, and deliberately so, but we also have some electronic technology. I'm not opposed to modern technology. I love it. We have a GPS chart plotter/depth sounder. I also have a handheld GPS with inbuilt charts for backup. And as further backup I have two GPS apps on a tablet. In future I would never buy a dedicated GPS chart plotter because I think the tablet apps, which are literally cheaper than a pizza, are just as good. It's scary to think that one of these apps contains all the marine charts from the Ross Sea to Samoa.

I've been fascinated by GPS ever since it became available. I got my first handheld one for sea kayaking in 1996. It still works well, though its functions are extremely limited in comparison with today's models.

My history studies took me back to the early navigational techniques of both Polynesian and European explorers. With regard to the latter, the development of the chronometer by John Harrison, so well summarised in Dava Sobel's *Longitude,* enthralled me.

I often pondered what Cook might have done with a GPS. I actually attended a talk by John Robson on that exact topic. His conclusion shocked the audience, though it was perfectly obvious if one thought carefully about it. Cook, said Robson, would not have been a better navigator had he had one. To be sure he would have always known where he was, there would have been a track of his travels, and he would have fixed and charted any land he came to. But then he did this anyway with remarkable accuracy. For example, his chart of the Firth of Thames would not have been better had he had a GPS.

A GPS actually has quite limited use unless you know where you are going to and what is there. Because Cook was among the first of the Pacific's western explorers, no GPS could have told him what to expect and where. A chart can only first exist after the event, not before it. Certainly a GPS would have saved Cook thousands of hours of complex mathematical calculations, and for that he would have been grateful.

The sounder is mainly used to get our anchoring depths. I also carry a lead line on a hand-fishing spool. There's something basic and satisfying about lowering a lump of lead on a marked line to the bottom. Utterly reliable.

Electronic devices can never be totally reliable. And if they don't work they simply create anger and frustration. If all our electrics go down I have a good hand-bearing compass that can clip into a holder on the cabin top. If I break or drop that overboard I have a simple, bomb-proof hiker compass. In zero visibility as long as I know where west is I will hit land.

While all my navigation, or rather pilotage, is using a GPS, and the no.1 eyeball, I sometimes take three bearings on the hand-bearing compass and mark them on the chart, just for old times' sake. Not too much mental agility is needed to add 20 degrees (east variation) to the magnetic bearing before marking the true bearing on the chart. Normally the GPS is most useful for giving the boat speed, and also for indicating if we are heading towards some dreaded sunken rock.

We carry a full set of paper charts of the Gulf and beyond. I love them. But I have to admit that they probably get more use on wet winter's days at home when I spread them on the lounge floor and dream.

I like making little electronic devices. I have a very simple water alarm in the bilge – when moisture connects two bared wires a piezo alarm run from a nine-volt battery shatters the silence. I have also fitted a thermal switch onto the engine exhaust at the saltwater elbow so a few seconds after the cooling water stops flowing (or doesn't start) a circuit is closed and another alarm goes off, and long before the freshwater coolant heats up to set off the inbuilt engine overheating alarm. I built our LED reading lights, and our LED anchor light.

We have a Personal Locator Beacon (PLB) with a built-in GPS. If it is set off, satellites inform the relevant rescue centre of where and who we are. There's a fixed VHF radio plus a handheld backup, and a SW portable radio receiver (with Single Side Band) for those marine forecasts from Taupo Maritime Radio when in remote, land-locked anchorages sheltered from VHF reception.

There's also a good old-fashioned brass barometer, and a matching brass tide clock.

Western imagining[4]

Islands, like boats, are not just physical objects but ideas and emotions. The Western view of islands is cultural more than it is geographic. Judeo-Christian tradition had men and women created in Paradise, specifically the Garden of Eden. They behaved badly and were driven out. The idea of an earthly Paradise lasted for a long time in Christian doctrines. But where was it? No one ever found it in the known world of Europe, but with the expansion of Europe overseas to the unknown world, to the Americas and beyond, perhaps it might be there? At the heart of the expansion of Spain, Portugal, Holland, France and England lay the search for Eden and, increasingly, hoped-for wealth. The earliest Spanish explorers in the Solomon Islands thought they had stumbled upon King Solomon's mines – hence the islands' name.

Even James Cook's voyages were in search of Terra Australis Incognita – the fabulously rich Great Unknown Southern Land. Cook disproved the existence of any such continent, but he and others did reveal many islands in the Pacific, and perhaps Paradise might be located there. A few initially thought it might be Tahiti. But of course that was no Paradise, nor were any other tropical islands (contrary to modern tourism hyperbole), nor was there fabulous wealth.

Yet tropical islands readily became entrenched in popular Western literature. Imagined islands soon became the site for a real or fantasy landscape of explorers, whalers, beachcombers and castaways, traders, pirates with wooden legs and parrots, swashbucklers, masters and commanders. Many youthful generations have been deeply influenced by Defoe's *Robinson Crusoe* and Stevenson's *Treasure Island*. Films like *Moby Dick* and various versions of *Mutiny on the Bounty* have also fired young imaginations.

All these matters are set deep in Western imaginations. We grow up with the idea of small islands as familiar and exciting places, even if we have never been on one.

And islands are also psychological spaces, offering the promise of safety, as well as the promise of travel and adventure. Children are often attracted to the idea of islands, a form of enclosed place, like a hidey-hole, or tree hut.

Even as Western adults we have a fascination for being abandoned on a remote desert island which probably relates to fundamental human questions – who are we as individuals when stripped of the usual trappings of our society? Which is why I think a growling monster high-speed launch which brings all these trappings is such an anomaly in a quiet, bush-surrounded anchorage in a place like Port

FitzRoy or Moturekareka.

We in Auckland are lucky that the Hauraki Gulf, and the Bay of Islands, offer us ready and unique access to large numbers of small islands, and if we are honest with ourselves, the attraction is ultimately rooted in our cultural memory and expectation, as much as it is in the modern recreational possibilities that these islands offer.

We smile when we see dolphins. We smile when we approach and land on islands.

Western naming

All humans see and know things culturally. Places are usually accorded names. To name a new place is an act of possession because it gives it an immediate cultural familiarity. It makes the unknown knowable and thus potentially controllable.

Western explorers in New Zealand (and elsewhere) typically gave new places names that were commonly derived from locations in their home countries. So, for example, Cook bestowed the name River Thames on our Firth of Thames and Waihou River. Names of official figures frequently appear on his early charts. In the Gulf we find Point Rodney and Cape Colvill [sic]. Sometimes he gave places names to signify their (to him) obvious characteristics, hence Barrier Isles (Great and Little Barrier). Sometimes, but not often, he named places on whimsy – the Hen and Chicken Islands, the Aldermen Islands, the Poor Knights. Later explorers and travellers continued this process of naming.

During the early colonial era there was a heavy overlay of Western place naming, and, in the Gulf, a good deal of it was naval-related, with names of captains and their vessels and admirals. Thus, for example, the channels we know as Blanche and Rosario came from warships of those names. Challenger Island, Jellicoe, Craddock, Colville and Parry Channels derive from admirals' names. Coromandel and Miranda were named after warships. Then there is Man of War Bay on Waiheke, and Man of War passage on Great Barrier.

There are names from sea captains (e.g. Burgess Bay and Burgess Island, Fairchild Reef), and traders (e.g. Browns Island, Nagle Cove, Port Abercrombie); and administrators and politicians (e.g. Mount Hobson, Port FitzRoy, Grey Group Islands).

There's a particular concentration of colonial power names as you arrive at Great Barrier to enter Port FitzRoy, initially passing through the Grey Group Islands, then through the Man of War passage into Port FitzRoy, and high above is Mount Hobson. The narrow channel immediately after the Man of War passage is called Governors Pass. British warrior heroes are remembered in nearby locations off the western end of Kaikoura Island with Wellington Head and Nelson Island.

European names in the Hauraki Gulf are overwhelmingly English, though the French explorer Dumont d'Urville who visited the Gulf in 1827 named the sharp rocks at the northern end of Great Barrier Island Pointe de Aiguilles – the Needles. He also saw some rocks out from Whangaparapara on Great Barrier Island that reminded him of canoes with sails – thus Pirogues (though they appear on the charts now as Piroque, and also as The Pigeons). We also have D'Urville Rocks off the northern coast of Waiheke, though this name appears on later charts of others but not on his own.

One pleasing and perhaps surprising characteristic of colonial place naming in New Zealand is that so many existing Maori names were retained, a lot more perhaps, than indigenous names in most other settler colonies. In recent years some Maori names have returned to replace or be alternatives to formerly imposed European names – notably Aotea for Great Barrier Island, Hauturu for Little Barrier Island, and Motukorea for Browns Island.

Maori naming and imagining

Maori explorers, like western explorers, commonly gave names that derived from their former homelands to newly discovered places. Tiritiri Matangi and Motutapu are two Hauraki Gulf examples. Figures from their past were also used in naming places, whether they were deities, explorers and founding figures actual or mythical, or ancestors. Such names were usually associated with some activity or event involving the person, and were not, as in the case of Cook, just taken from some list of people who lived on the other side of the world that he felt obliged to honour.

Sometimes places reminded Maori of everyday things or objects. Various Gulf islands were referred to as floats of the fishing nets of legendary figures. Motuora was an anchor. Some islands are regarded as scales from the giant fish that Maui hauled up – Te Ika a Maui, or the North Island. Bird life commonly inspired names. Motukorea/Browns Island means island of oystercatchers. Kawau is a place of shags, Motutara a place of kahawai birds, or white-fronted terns.

Or names came from the attributes of a place. Great Barrier Island was Aotea, meaning literally land of white cloud, or the place or source of light, since the dawn breaks from that direction.

Given the maritime nature of the Gulf's early human inhabitants, wind conditions were as significant then as now for sailors. Tiritiri Matangi means windy place, Little Barrier Island or Hauturu means resting place of winds. The name Hauraki itself means an unpleasant north wind, though it may also refer to the periodic waves of Ngā Puhi invaders coming down from Northland driven by such winds.

What we now call the Hauraki Gulf was Tīkapa Moana, meaning the sea crossed by a great many canoes since it was a major intersection for those travelling north or south, or from the east to the west coast of the North Island via portages across the Auckland isthmus, or Tāmaki Makau Rau.

But there are dangers in always assuming literal translations of names for 'meanings'. And there are often multiple, even sometimes contradictory, names and meanings over time for different groups of people. A fine account of Hauraki Gulf Maori place names is Taimoana Tūroa's *Te Takoto o te Whenua o Hauraki. Hauraki Landmarks*, edited by Te Ahukaramū Charles Royal.

Maori history and culture is ultimately bound to genealogy or whakapapa. Relationships form the narrative backbone of the past, going back to the creation. This narrative overlays the landscape in which events took place.

Places can thus be understood not just as physical locations, but read as history, as sites of ancestral people and activities as well as current homes of self, friends or enemies. As Peter McBurney notes: 'ancient traditions are not simply quaint fairytales; they are site specific narratives about particular ancestors and are rich with cultural references. As such they are an integral part of the cultural fabric binding the people to the land and the sea.'[5]

There are vast numbers of examples, but let two geographic clusters of names suffice here: the *Tainui* canoe struck a sandbank near Devonport. A tohunga called Taikehu climbed out and pushed the canoe to deeper water – the sandbank was named after him. He also called the three peaks of Rangitoto the dorsal fins of Taiheku, and named Motutapu after his ancestral homeland in tropical Polynesia.[6]

The Coromandel Peninsula is replete with ancestral significance. The mountain of Moehau at the end of the Peninsula that dominates the entire Gulf is known as the windy sleeping place of Tamatekapua, the chief of the *Arawa* canoe. He had chosen this site for his burial when the *Arawa* had first sailed around the tip of the Peninsula. That is one reason why no climbers are allowed on the summit today.

Another story is that the whole of the Peninsula represents a mighty canoe – the prow is Mt Te Aroha, the stern piece is Moehau. The mountains in between represent the crew. From a distance at sea, say from the Kawau region, this is just how it looks, once you think about it, even if you can't see all the way to the prow. Even the mountains seem to nod with each paddle stroke. It's not what you look at, it's what you see.

Yet another tale is that the Peninsula is the spine of Maui's fish or Te Ika a Maui, which some think was a stingray.[7]

Many 19th century Maori also believed that the Coromandel ranges were a location of numerous and often scary spirit beings. For example, Castle Rock, that excellent navigation marker en route to Coromandel Harbour, was haunted by Mahoao, white-skinned creatures like men but with gleaming tusks and yellow hair. They went about sweetly calling haere mai and anyone who came near was devoured.

Maori (and Polynesian) perceptions of landscape still reflect a dynamically lived cultural significance. The places they see and imagine are alive with intimate human and animal associations both mythically, historically and temporally. In the Hauraki Gulf and throughout New Zealand, there is not a place or feature of the landscape or creature that does not have a living past in the present. But this process should not be romanticised. Like human homes and homelands everywhere they were also locations of universal human behaviour – including greed, vengeance, power seeking and brutal conflict, and oral tradition reflects on these matters too.

A dynamic past[8]

A history of pre-European peoples in the Hauraki Gulf is the story, firstly, of arrivals from distant lands, then, increasingly, migrations from neighbouring regions in New Zealand, creating an ongoing jostling of groups keen to dominate and exploit the Gulf's rich land and marine resources. It's a complex narrative, particularly given the changing dynamics not just of conflicts but also of alliances and intermarriages and overlapping claims. Allies might readily become enemies, and vice versa. This past, like all human pasts, cannot be easily described since there was no status quo.

According to legend, amongst the earliest people in the Hauraki Gulf, here before the arrival of the celebrated migratory canoes, was Ngāti Hako.

Mainstream Maori traditions of the Hauraki Gulf region revolve around the later arrival of several key ancestral canoes. The specific detail may or may not relate to actual historical events, but the legends have an actuality in that all Maori tribes have specific identities and traditions that usually start with canoe arrivals, and we know that peoples from southern tropical Polynesia did of course arrive in a number of large waka over a period of time.

Legend tells that among the earliest major canoes that came into the Gulf, at about the same time, were *Tainui* and *Arawa*. *Arawa,* travelling from the Bay of Plenty, explored the Hauraki Gulf and Waitemata Harbour before ending up back at Maketu in the Bay of Plenty. *Tainui* on its coastal explorations sailed into the Waitemata Harbour, rested at Duders Beach in Devonport, then sailed up the Tamaki River. It was portaged across to the Manukau Harbour and ended its journey at Kawhia on the west coast.

Arawa descendants predominated in the Gulf for some 300 years, outnumbering some residual Tainui members, as well as some of the settlers who predated both *Arawa* and *Tainui* canoes. The main tribal groups were Te Patukirikiri, Ngāti Hako, Ngāti Huarere, Ngāti Hei, Ngāi Tai, Ngāti Pūkenga and Ngāti Rāhiri. These are referred to as the Hauraki tribes.

Round about the end of the 1500s, *Tainui* descendants began arriving from the Waikato region in some numbers and by about 1700 they had created a kind of federation called Marutūahu that through conquest and diplomacy took precedence, but not complete control, over much of Hauraki. These tribes were Ngāti Rongoū, Ngāti Tamaterā, Ngāti Whanaunga, Ngāti Maru and Ngāti Pāoa.

The outer islands of the Gulf were occupied by Ngāti Wai, out of the Whangarei area.

A branch of Ngāti Whātua established itself on part of the Tamaki isthmus from its more immediate homelands in Northland.

At about the time of European contact a very simplified, and contested, list of broad groups in the Hauraki Gulf region would be:

Hauraki tribes – Te Patukirikiri, Ngāti Hako, Ngāti Huarere, Ngāti Hei, Ngāi Tai, Ngāti Pūkenga and Ngāti Rāhiri.
Marutūahu confederation – Ngāti Rongoū, Ngāti Tamaterā, Ngāti Whanaunga, Ngāti Maru, Ngāti Patukirikiri and Ngāti Pāoa.
Tamaki isthmus tribes – Ngāti Pāoa, Ngāi Tai, Te Wai-o-Hua, Ngāti Whātua-o-Tamaki, Ngāti Te Ata and Kawerau.
Mahurangi region – Kawerau a Maki
Outer Gulf – Ngāti Wai

In terms of customary rights a much simplified, and also contested, guide for about the time of early Western contact is:

Great Barrier – Ngāti Wai/Marutūahu
Little Barrier/Mokohinau/Poor Knights/ Hen and Chicken Islands – Ngāti Wai
Kawau – Ngāti Wai/Ngāti Pāoa/NgāiTai/Kawerau
Tiritiri Matangi – Kawerau/Ngāti Pāoa
Motutapu – Ngāi Tai/Hauraki/Ngāti Pāoa
Rakino – Ngāti Pāoa
Motuihe – Ngāi Tai, Ngāti Pāoa
Rangitoto – Ngāi Tai, Ngāti Pāoa
Browns – Ngāti Tamaterā
Rotoroa/Pakatoa –Ngāti Pāoa/Ngāi Tai
Ponui – Ngāti Pāoa/Ngāi Tai
Waiheke – Ngāti Pāoa/Ngāti Maru/Patukirikiri
Auckland isthmus and surrounds – Ngāti Pāoa, Ngāi Tai, Te Wai-o-Hua, Ngāti Whātua-o-Tamaki, Ngāti Te Ata and Kawerau
Mahurangi region – Kawerau a Maki

In times of peace, especially, there was much mobility and flexibility at the local level, with people travelling to other places, for social reasons, to negotiate rights to use some resource, and to trade and exchange goods and produce. Subtribes or hapu always had a considerable measure of independence of action. And there were many more groups developing, splitting and moving about than the simple charts above indicate. Groups did not stay rigidly within their territories, nor were they subject to some centralised system of conformity and control. The modern-day major iwi have, or claim to have, a much more monolithic (and often corporate) view of themselves than traditionally was the case. In brief, it was a socio-political patchwork of dynamic change and complexity.

One of the most insightful descriptions of traditional Maori society is still that given by Joseph-Paul Gaimard, Dumont D'Urville's naturalist, in 1827:

> *These two great islands have no one chief exercising authority over a large area. The land is divided into innumerable tribes, each with its own chief who is independent of his neighbours. This chief, far from having absolute power over those he governs, appears to have no authority beyond what public opinion accords him; and, in any case, cannot force a free man to do anything against his will … Thus each tribe constitutes a sort of little republic, which will sometimes join with others in a federation of a temporary character, when all will obey one chief for purposes of war …* [9]

Tenuous connections

I have an utterly tenuous connection to the *Tainui* canoe. When I was at Vauxhall primary school we were all divided into 'houses', each having a Maori name – Arawa, Tainui, Ngapuhi (as it was then spelt) and

Rewi. In 1959 I was house captain of Tainui. In that year a memorial was opened at Duders Beach, where the *Tainui* canoe is supposed to have landed briefly during its exploration of the Waitemata Harbour. As captain of the Tainui house at school, I took some very minor part in the opening. I have no recollection of what I did but I remember being there.

The memorial is still there, of course, notable for the bronze replica of the korotangi, a carved pigeon-like bird made of serpentine that legend claims came on the *Tainui* canoe from Polynesia. The 'original' artefact first appeared in Cambridge in the Waikato in the 1870s and had allegedly been found at Aotea Harbour, which is near the claimed resting place of the *Tainui*. It became a revered object amongst Tainui people, was deposited in the Dominion Museum and has recently been returned to Tainui as part of a Treaty of Waitangi settlement.

Its provenance is actually quite uncertain, and controversial. It is not a Polynesian carving, serpentine is found worldwide, and it is even entirely possible that it was some sort of European or Oriental ornament brought to New Zealand in 19th century colonial baggage.

The memorial is quite tasteful, as memorials go. It is a simple wall-like structure of white stone with two large bronze plaques, one in English, the other Maori, telling the story of the Great Migration and the arrival of *Tainui* carrying the korotangi. The bird itself is mounted on a bronze orb, atop a short central column. The whole is set under two large pohutukawa. It's a beautiful location.

And I have another even more tenuous connection with *Tainui*. I once took part in an annual organised Round Auckland sea kayak trip. Starting at St Heliers, we followed the path of the legendary canoe, paddling up the Tamaki River and portaging to the Manukau Harbour. Whereas *Tainui* was dragged over muddy tracks and through scrub, we wheeled our craft along streets in state house areas and across the railway yard over-bridge to the now mangrove-choked Manukau shoreline. We did not follow *Tainui* out across the bar into the Tasman but we did another portage at Green Bay to the Whau River, and returned to St Heliers, completing a circumnavigation of the city.

Musket wars

After several centuries of initial colonisation of the new land and with an increasing population, Maori began to develop more organised communities with their own identities and territories and thus lay the very early bases for the territorial claims and tribal groupings that exist today. As mentioned previously, there was much jostling for resources in the Gulf and Auckland area generally.

There were also regular attacks on the region from outsiders and counter attacks during the 18th century. In particular there was much ill feeling between Ngā Puhi, who were becoming dominant in Northland, and Ngāti Whātua and the Marutūahu tribes, especially Ngāti Pāoa. In the early 1790s Ngā Puhi attacked Ngāti Pāoa in battles at Takapuna, Waiheke and the Tamaki River, and were finally repulsed. In return Ngāti Pāoa and Ngāti Maru raided the Bay of Islands and inflicted defeat on Ngā Puhi. There were portents here for the future.

But it was another 20 years before the Auckland region was again invaded from the north. This was the time when Maori started to exploit the opportunities offered by European contact, especially new crops such as potatoes that could be grown more easily and cropped heavier than kumara, and other vegetables and also pigs. While most direct contact with Westerners was in the Bay of Islands, such items soon found their way, indirectly at first, into the Auckland, Coromandel and Bay of Plenty regions. The sale of pigs and potatoes to European ships enabled Bay of Islands Maori to be the first to acquire muskets. Northern raiders became adept at capturing large numbers of prisoners, some from as far away as Bay of Plenty and East Cape, to work the potato fields to pay for more muskets.

The first of the major Ngā Puhi musket raids came in 1821. Hongi Hika organised 2000 fighters with 1000 muskets and with a flotilla of some 50 war canoes set out seeking vengeance against Ngāti Pāoa and Ngāti Maru. The first people to be attacked were on the Mahurangi coast, Whangaparaoa and Takapuna, as well Ngāti Pāoa on Kawau and Tiritiri Matangi. But the main targets were the two large Ngāti Pāoa pa on the Tamaki River – Mauinaina and Mokoia. Estimates of those killed range up to 3000. Those who could fled far inland. Hongi then descended upon the Ngāti Maru pa at Te Totara, near Thames, and there was more killing. In all some 2000 captives were taken back to the Bay of Islands.

The next year Hongi's target was the Waikato people. The great Matakitaki pa, in the upper Waipa area, was taken with several thousand killed. In 1823 Hongi turned his attention, with similar results, to the tribes of Rotorua.

Finally, in 1825 Hongi turned on Ngāti Whatūa, whose Tamaki members to this point had evaded his attacks on Auckland isthmus largely by being absent from there during his previous raids. Joining their Kaipara members they engaged with Hongi at Te Ika-a-Ranginui, not far from Kaiwaka. It was another rout. Those who remained in Tamaki wisely moved away before Hongi could get at them too.

Thus had Hongi effectively destroyed the power of most of the pre-musket era tribes in Hauraki/Tamaki.

Dumont d'Urville sailed about the Hauraki Gulf and Waitemata Harbour in 1827, reporting:

> *We did not notice any trace of inhabitants, nothing but one or two fires a very long way off in the interior. There can be no doubt that this extreme depopulation is due to the ravages of war … The natives of Shouraki are engaged in continuous warfare with the tribes from the north, who come to ravage their territory every year. – Firearms give an enormous advantage to the latter.*[10]

The landscape was empty, not because everyone had been killed but because nobody dared live there, such was the damage and grief caused by Hongi.

Kawau, Tiritiri Matangi, and most of the inner Gulf islands were completely abandoned.

As the Maori possession of muskets filtered further southwards, so was the rest of the North Island, the South Island and even the Chatham Islands convulsed by warfare and forced migration for another decade. Eventually Maori mutual possession of firearms, war and migration weariness, plus the opportunities they saw with new European influences ranging from commerce to Christianity, began to change some traditional values.

The further story of the Hauraki/Tamaki tribes in the later 1820s and 1830s is one largely of exile, further rivalry and fighting. Not until the mid-to-later 1830s were there serious attempts to return to former lands. Many people never did and settled in far-off places. When people did return, it was not to the same world. Not only had the old world of Maori politics and relationships changed, but their former lands were now sites of growing western commerce and influence. Some took the chance to assert sometimes dubious claims of former occupation in order to enhance potential new commercial opportunities, including possible land selling. Ngāti Pāoa were particularly active with their 'expansionism' in the inner Gulf in the 1830s. By the time of official colonisation they may sometimes have made some rather optimistic ownership claims?

One of the great problems for the modern-day Treaty policy of trying to solve historical grievances, especially relating to loss of land after 1840, is the fact that Maori claims and rights to territorial occupation in the two decades before 1840 were profoundly upset by their own political convulsions during the musket wars. There was in effect no agreed status quo existing in 1840. The Treaty claim process, however, takes 1840 as a base line. Deciding what this is or was, can sometimes be problematic.

Motutapu

Motutapu was a name brought from Polynesia, meaning sacred place and home of Tinirau, the god of fish. There were a number of Motutapu locations in eastern Polynesia, typically small islands close to centres of population where arriving voyagers could rest and be protected, and also controlled if need be, before being accepted into the wider community.

The extent to which the Hauraki Gulf Motutapu actually performed this role is conjecture, for its human history, like that of its island neighbours, seems more about occupations and occasional conquests. Its fortified pa sites as well as its European fortifications derive from its commanding position overlooking the whole of the inner Hauraki Gulf. All this indicates a history of some uncertainty for both Maori and Pakeha.

Ngāi Tai were the island's main occupants from early settlement times, with some later groups such as Hauraki and Ngāti Pāoa having an occasional presence. In the 1830s Ngāi Tai sold it to Europeans who farmed it until WWI when it came under Crown ownership. In the mid-19th century the then-owner Robert Graham introduced a range of exotic animals (as George Grey was also doing on Kawau) including wallabies, deer, emu, pheasants, quail, sheep and cattle. Emu Bay and Emu Point, were, however, named after a vessel named *Emu* ran aground there. Motutapu became part of the Hauraki Gulf Maritime Park in 1967.

From a distance at sea the island is low, looks mostly treeless, and is very green in winter and burnished gold in summer. Some 500,000 trees have been planted by the very active Motutapu Restoration Society, 50 per cent more than on Tiritiri Matangi, yet such is the size of the island that most of the planting is not always obvious from the sea. Most of the trees have been planted in the gullies, such as behind Home Bay, and so do not appear on the skyline. Nor will they do so since to protect Maori and European heritage large areas of this island will be left unplanted. So it looks a bit unprepossessing, yet its landscape is packed with interest.

Rangitoto and Motutapu are joined by a causeway built during WWII. To its northern side there is a large area between the two islands that dries out at low tide. On the south side lies Islington Bay – the only reliable anchorage. It used to be called Drunken Bay since ships' captains used to round up their boozed crews in Auckland and sober them up in the bay before heading out to sea. It can now be an impossibly crowded anchorage in summer. Its worst feature is the bottom sediment of the stickiest goop that fouls anchor warps, chains and anchors. It's that 600-year-old Rangitoto ash. A bucket on the bow and a brush is required equipment, and even then there's usually a sticky, slimy black mess left on the foredeck.

Around Emu Point and across Emu Bay there can be difficult tidal currents. Emu Bay was the site of the first main island homestead, built by the Reid family. They built another one, now restored, a bit further on in Home Bay.

Home Bay features a huge campground, though you need a private boat to get there (or else a very long walk from the ferry at Islington Bay wharf). It has long been a great picnic spot. The Reids hosted annual grand gatherings in Edwardian times. On one notable day in February 1903 some 14,000 Aucklanders, about 14 per cent of Auckland's population, arrived in fleets of steamers. Others came from far away including 100 on the train from Waihi.

> *The high hills in the background were not burned up, as is usual at this season of the year, and the white tents of the stall keepers, the varied and beautiful dresses of the ladies, all served to make the surroundings of Mr Reid's beautiful home resemble more a gala day at the Auckland Domain than an island 16 miles from the city.*[11]

Old photographs often show the bay more crowded with yachts and launches than it is today.

The island's eastern and northern sides feature pleasingly sculptured greywacke shorelines, unlike the south western side where there are high and brittle sedimentary cliffs. In a south-westerly wind, the small inlets of Mullet Bay and Station Bay are great anchorages. I prefer Station Bay since its protective point is a wonderful fortified pa site with highly visible defensive ditches. If the yacht lies the right way at anchor I can lie on my bunk and see the pa and imagine all sorts of ancient activity. It looks particularly haunting in moonlight.

Around the corner, along the northern coastline, is the excellent deep-water anchorage of Waikalabubu Bay, and at the north-western tip of the island is Billy Goat Point with a prominent WWII concrete bunker in ironic complement to the Station Bay pa site.

We don't like sailing close by the island's reef-strewn western coastline.

Motutapu provides some of the very best walking of anywhere near Auckland for those who like to stride out. The island is criss-crossed with tracks, mostly over open farmland. No part of the island is off limits. Apart from the few Department of Conservation metalled roads, the tracks are mainly unformed, though well marked with poles. You can walk large numbers of kilometres if you want to (the island is over seven kilometres north/south), and remember the island also links over the causeway with the roads and tracks on Rangitoto.

There are no cars to bother about, apart from the occasional Department of Conservation utes on the roads, no dogs and mostly very few other walkers. But there are sometimes cattle who will want to follow you but will always get out of your way if you walk purposefully.

The tracks along the island's many ridges give unforgettable 360-degree views over the Gulf. Those who are lucky enough to get there on their own boat will find tracks leading up to the main ridges from all the usual anchorages. Those who take the infrequent ferry to Islington Bay will have to start from there. And you will have to have your own food and water, though drinking water is available at Home Bay.

We have a number of favourite walking destinations depending where we anchor. Billy Goat Point at the northern end features craggy cliff-top views and marvellous pohutukawa seemingly growing out of rock, not to mention WWII defensive pill boxes and related structures. The main war remnants are the three Mark 21 naval gun emplacements on the island's high point, recently cleaned up and open for public viewing. On the site are also all sorts of observation posts, anti-aircraft and radar installation remains, long underground stairways and underground storage rooms.

Of course the naval guns themselves are very long gone. But they have been recreated in a short film made by Chris Keenan and staff from the Department of Conservation entitled the 'Guns of Motutapu' complete with 3D animation. This is usually continuously shown at the Department of Conservation's mini-theatre near the summit of North Head, Devonport. Other remains of WWII military activity can be found in many places on the island.

There are also some notable locations of pre-European Maori settlement, perhaps the most striking being the defensive pa at Station Bay. But for me the most fascinating, even though there is nothing to see, is the site where the hundreds of 1400AD human and dog footprints were found in the ash from Rangitoto as it was erupting. The site, known as the Sunde site, named after the archaeologist who found them, is at a small beach sometimes called West Point beach (though it has other names too), located roughly halfway between Administration Bay and the causeway. It is accessible from both places by tracks. Boat access is also possible, but yachts will have to anchor some way offshore to avoid extensive drying reefs that run along the coastline. I prefer the overland route.

It's a nice sandy beach backed by a small area of flat land, surrounded by densely overgrown high ground. Of course you cannot see the footprints or even work out where they might be, unless you are with an archaeologist. The flat area is heavily covered in almost impenetrable, waist high kikuyu grass and scrub. You can see some casts of the footprints in the Auckland Museum. But I have stood on the beach and gazed across to Rangitoto, less than two kilometres away, and tried to imagine what it must have been like watching the new island steam and boil its way out of the sea, its lava spewing. The noise, smoke, ash-fall, smell and volcanic fireworks must have been both spectacular and terrifying. It's not hard to envisage groups of locals standing on this beach, awestruck, sometimes crying out in amazement or fear, children yelling, dogs howling – for Polynesian dogs could not bark.

Motutapu - WWII

Amongst my mum's few possessions when she died at 96 was a notebook in which she had laboriously copied in pencil full instructions for plotting a target ship and firing the naval guns on Motutapu. It's an old-fashioned schooled writing – letters all nicely rounded, neat and tidy. There's no crossing out. On the faded cover are the smudged letters:

810272 Gunn Howe, R.V.
66th Battery
9th Heavy Rgt

When my dad went off to war with the 24th Battalion in 1940, my mum joined the Women's Auxiliary Army Corp (WAACS). She was first taught how to drive a truck (and she kept her heavy traffic licence until well into her 80s), and then was sent to Motutapu and became a gunner, alternating between spotting and plotting from the summit of Rangitoto and manning the guns on Motutapu.

The notes seem impossibly technical and packed with acronyms – BPR, FDT, CBC, CC, FTD, PF and dozens more. The 46 pages of instructions are precise, yet obscure from this distance. One small example:

Dumaresq is key of FDT is operated by plotting officer to set the Dumaresq for inclination or course and speed. Target ship is rotated by inclination handle wheel for required inclination or course. To set speed turn speed hand wheel till boss in centre of the ship reaches required speed.

A Dumaresq, I found when I looked it up, was invented in 1902 by a John Dumaresq of the Royal Navy. It was in essence a mechanical analogue computer that related gunfire controls to the movements of targets.

My mum was a small cog in the Fortress System which linked the gunners, spotters and plotters at Whangaparaoa, Castor Bay, Fort Takapuna, North Head, Bastion Point, Rangitoto, Motutapu and Waiheke.

The main Motutapu firepower consisted of three MK21 6 inch naval guns. They had a range of almost 30 kilometres with shells rising to 9000 metres. They were really all that could offer any opposition to any incoming Japanese warships. There were bigger guns on Whangaparaoa and Stony Batter on Waiheke but these were not commissioned until after the war. Had the Japanese arrived, as expected in 1942, they probably would have had an easy conquest, especially with their air power. By 1943 the imminent threat had passed, and there was at least the comfort of the arrival of US troops in large numbers in Auckland, some of them stationed in Islington Bay.

She spent some years on the island, along with 800 New Zealand defence personnel. There are numerous photographs of her with other WAACs and their male officers. She was less than 1.5 metres in height so her army fatigues always looked rather baggy, but in her well-tailored dress uniform she looked smart.

She never said much about her war years, but on a couple of occasions she told a few harmless stories, such as how one of her officers was named Keys, so the girls nicknamed him 'Buncha'. And there was the time that the guns fired many salvoes at a target barge towed well behind a launch out towards Tiritiri Matangi. The spotters failed to see any shots splashing in the vicinity, but then saw smoke rising from the nearby Noisies Islands which had been bombarded in error.

She once said that she was more worried about what was happening to my dad than about a Japanese attack. He had been landed in Greece and driven out, landed in Crete and driven out, and sent to North Africa where he was captured by the Germans at Sidi Rezegh. He was shipped across to Italy as one of 2000 prisoners on the vessel *Jantzen* and sunk by a British torpedo just off Cape Methoni. Some 500 were killed. He made it ashore and was incarcerated in Italy.

The missing-in-action telegram from the New Zealand government reached her in January 1942, and the telegram that he was a prisoner of war was in February 1942. In September 1943 another telegram advised her that he was prisoner of the Italians at C.C.P.G. 57, (Grupignano) Italy. She wrote on it, 'First news of Ken for 18 months.'

The Allies eventually advanced into Italy. One day the Italian guards all ran away. The prisoners were led to believe that the Americans would arrive the next day, so they stayed there. But that night the Germans rounded them up and took them in railway cattle trucks over the Alps. In January 1944 she was told that he was in Stalag 344, Upper Silesia, Poland. He was forced to work in coal mines. As the Russians advanced, he was one of 80,000 prisoners of war whom the Germans force-marched westwards across Poland, Czechoslovakia and into Germany in mid-winter. Thousands died. It is often referred to as the Death March. He returned to New Zealand. When he left he had tight curly hair. When he came back it was straight. My mum's first words on seeing him were 'What's happened to your hair?' He had been away for five years.

In her old age we got her back to the summit of Rangitoto when the tractor train started for tourists, as I've said, but we were unable to take her back to Motutapu.

My dad, who never set foot on the island, has a presence there through my mum's war posting. I always feel a bit dismal if walking about Administration Bay where the army barracks were located (and some are still used for the Outdoor Education Camp), and up the barren valley to the gun emplacements. Many of the ideals that my parents' generation suffered for in WWII are not much in evidence in the modern world.

Motutapu - life at Station Bay

It was one of Auckland's coldest winter days, a 20 knot southerly blowing directly off the snow-covered central North Island. My plan was to sail from Gulf Harbour, circumnavigate Rangitoto and spend the night at Station Bay on Motutapu's eastern side. I had with me in my tablet a long report complete with maps and photographs by archaeologist Janet Davidson on Maori settlement sites in Station Bay.[12] I intended to wander over these sites, which included a fortified pa.

The wind had been forecast to turn south-west, giving me a nice close reach, but it never did, and I ended up tacking into the head wind and tide for most of the day. At the Rangitoto beacon I looked forward to getting some wind on the beam as I turned eastwards, but true to form the wind swung to the south-east. I then noticed a small tear in the genoa so decided to call it a day at Islington Bay where I stuck some sail-repair tape over the rip. By then it was near dark and with the wind blowing directly into the bay I snuggled down for the night and looked at the maps and photographs again, thinking about Station Bay on neighbouring Motutapu.

I have often anchored at Station Bay and wandered about the pa headland, but not with this wealth of archaeological findings at my fingertips. It's a marvellous area for any human habitation, tucked just below the main island ridge and thus sheltered from south-westerly winds, with all-day sun, a few choice hill-top building sites, some flat areas with creeks, a small sandy beach, exposed reef areas and a sheltered cove.

At Vauxhall primary school we were taught how to make model Maori pa. We were each given a lump of green plasticine which we shaped like a hill and stuck it onto a board. Pa palisades were made from match sticks. The sea was painted blue. We made a beach (with real sand glued on) complete with tiny model canoes. We made little houses or whare out of sliced, soft inner core of flax wood. Station Bay is *exactly* like this.

The work of Davidson and others show that the bay was almost continuously occupied from before 1500. By the 17th century there were more permanent building sites and the fortified pa was built on the point. There were undefended habitation sites on the flat area behind the beach and up the ridges of the two rounded hills rising from the flat. The landscape of the bay, and the whole island, looked much as it does today. Most of the original bush cover was probably destroyed during the Rangitoto eruption, and with human settlement any regenerating bush was burned to encourage the growth of bracken fern for food and to clear areas for kumara gardening. Station Bay was ideal for gardening, and there was also a great deal of shellfish gathering and fishing, especially for snapper. Davidson concludes that it was 'a relatively stable and peaceful way of life, punctuated by periodic episodes of stress when the fortifications were built and rebuilt'.[13]

The archaeological diggings at Station Bay reveal some bone, shell and stone tools, including some obsidian from Te Ahumata on Great Barrier and lesser amounts from further away. Shellfish were pipi, cat's eye, cockles and tuatua, supplemented with numerous other species.

Fish was overwhelmingly snapper followed well down the list by gurnard, shark, barracouta, kahawai and others. The range of snapper sizes at any one time suggests extensive use of nets rather than reliance on hook-and-line fishing.

There was little sign of birds in the diet. Kiore and the Polynesian dog remains were present. Two apparently interred adult skeletons, one male, one female, were uncovered.

Next morning I sailed out of Islington Bay and passed this former Maori community at a bitterly cold Station Bay, noting the three hilltop sites from the Davidson maps. A north-east gale was now forecast so rather than wandering ashore through the freezing wet grass I wimped out and set sail for home.

I returned to Station Bay for an overnighter some weeks later. I clambered about the pa and the hillsides behind the bay. The deep fortification cuts around the pa have lost some of their visual impact being full of the bracken which also covers the pa site as a whole. As the sun lowered towards the skyline its rays shone parallel with the hill ridges leading down to the bay, dramatically highlighting the depressions of kumara pits and the levelled areas for houses. A former human landscape momentarily came to life.

Securing the Hauraki Gulf

Future aliens coming to see what remains of our extinct society would note a preponderance of military defensive remains and conclude that we had always been a very nervous and insecure lot.

There is barely a hill top or headland that Maori did not fortify during their exclusive time in New Zealand. And European colonists soon built their protective devices, such as the Albert Barracks in early Auckland, partial walls of which still remain on the Auckland University campus. Once perceived internal threats from Maori had ended by the 1870s, there were fears of overseas attack, by Russians.

There were several 'Russian scares' in the 1870s but the most 'serious' one was in 1885 and had to do with Anglo-Russian rivalry in Afghanistan. In response, large gun positions were established at Takapuna Head (along with the quaint Victorian-style Fort Takapuna building), North Head, Mt Victoria, Bastion Point and Resolution Point (above Parnell). Contrary to popular opinion, these were not the disappearing guns. They were installed a bit later. The restored one on North Head, with its subterranean tunnels, remains a popular attraction for kids with torches.

Invasion fears during WWI were relatively subdued. The real threat, the most serious since the Ngā Puhi musket raiders of the

1820s, came with WWII and especially with the Japanese conquest of South-east Asia.

By 1942-43 Auckland and the Hauraki Gulf had a significant array of defensive measures. The details are very well described in Peter Corbett's *A First Class Defended Port*. The mainland remains are very familiar to all Aucklanders, and boaties see them all the time on the islands. Major gun emplacements linked by the Fortress System were on the Whangaparaoa Peninsula, Castor Bay, Takapuna Head, North Head, Mt Victoria, Bastion Point, Motutapu and Waiheke. There were smaller batteries in other locations.

Large numbers of concrete pill boxes were built as lookout posts and machine-gun positions. They are variously located on most of the Gulf islands from the outermost ones like Great Barrier and Mokohinau with many more of them closer in. There is a particularly heavy infestation on cliffs at every North Shore beach. The only use most of them got was when post-war North Shore teenagers, in pre-car days, went about their first amorous fumblings in the dank air.

There were radar stations, built a bit later in the war, at Bream Head, Mokohinau, Tiritiri Matangi, Cape Colville and Great Barrier (Moors Peak, Nagle Cove). Radar eventually replaced the mainly eye-ball-operated Fortress System.

A large magazine complex was built in Islington Bay, its remnants still very visible.

What are no longer visible are the sea-based defensive measures ringing the inner Gulf. Between Whangaparaoa and Tiritiri Matangi was a controlled minefield. This consisted of 18 loops each with 16 mines that could be detonated remotely to destroy both ships and submarines. From Tiritiri Matangi to the Noisies was a string of 400 contact mines. There were 16 contact mines between the Noisies and Rakino, and another six between Rakino and Motutapu.

There was a controlled minefield at Port Abercrombie and Man of War Passage to protect Port FitzRoy on Great Barrier Island.

Not all mines were recovered when clearing took place, some 50 sank. Some have been found later. As recently as 2014 four of them were found by US navy divers on the seabed.[14]

Seabed indicator loops, long coils of copper cables that measured magnetic change if a ship or submarine crossed them, were deployed in the Whangaparaoa Passage, near the big contact minefield between Tiritiri Matangi and the Noisies, east of Rakino and in the Motuihe and Rangitoto Channels.

ASDIC or sonar arrays that could pick up ships or submarines were near the big minefield, east of Rakino, and in the Motuihe and Rangitoto Channels.

The harbour entrance had some underwater hydrophones. A steel boom ran from North Head to Bastion Point.

Cliff-top searchlights could rake the Whangaparaoa Passage, Rangitoto Channel and harbour entrance. The concrete structure visible on Billy Goat Point, Motutapu, housed one of the lights.

It was unlikely that an enemy ship or submarine could have arrived unknown in the inner Gulf. Defences against aircraft attack were more problematic. Most anti-aircraft batteries were on the mainland and were primarily intended to protect munitions dumps, the Devonport Naval base and the Hobsonville and Whenuapai airfields.

How effective these defences would have been against mass Japanese aircraft was never tested. When a Japanese plane from two submarines (I-25 and I-21) flew over Auckland in broad daylight in March and May 1942 they were spotted but nobody took the slightest notice. Neither submarine was detected.

There was much public concern over the sinking of the *Niagara* between Whangarei and the Mokohinau Islands in 1940. The German raider *Orion* had laid 228 contact mines in three groups – from Cuvier to the Mercury Islands, from Cuvier to Great Barrier, and from Great Barrier to the Hen and Chickens. The *Niagara* hit one in the latter field, as did the coastal vessel *Puriri* sent to search for further mines. Coast watchers on Great Barrier Island actually spotted the *Orion* heading over the horizon the afternoon before it laid its mines that night. The then young Fred Medland, out coast watching with his father (John), still remembers the moment. That same night HMNZS *Achilles* was anchored in Port FitzRoy.

In the same year another raider, *Komet*, sank the *Holmwood* near the Chatham Islands and the *Rangitane* well out from East Cape. A third raider, *Adjutant*, laid mines off Lyttelton and Port Nicholson in 1941, though nobody knew until after the war.

In 1945 a German submarine, U-862, snooped close in and undetected around Great Barrier, Gisborne and Napier. There's even a story that some crew members sneaked ashore somewhere to get fresh milk. There are a number of anecdotes about submarine sightings along the Northland coast during the war, including at Great Barrier Island.

The best military intelligence even at the height of anxiety in 1942, and confirmed subsequently, was that it was unlikely Japan would ever mount a full-scale invasion. New Zealand was just too far away and did not have the resources required to fuel Japan's military-industrial demands. Those resources came instead from China and South-east Asia. Invasion by Germany was an unlikely possibility. It was too focused on Europe and Russia, and, in any case, had lost all its extensive, strategic Pacific colonies of Nauru, Marshall Islands, Caroline Islands, Mariana Islands, New Guinea and German Samoa during WWI. Germany mostly left the Pacific region to the Japanese once Japan entered the war.

Yet some sort of nasty attack, most likely by Japan, was still possible, as happened to Australia. The Allied military planners could never know for sure what might happen, and so had to take all possible precautions. But by 1943 fears of attack had subsided. The Japanese were now on the defensive in the Pacific. Plans for further Auckland defences were mostly deferred or shelved. Minefields were cleared, the harbour boom removed.

Sailing about the Hauraki Gulf islands offers plenty of opportunities to see and to visit former defensive positions. The Rangitoto summit has spotting and plotting rooms, there's the old munitions base in Islington Bay, and on Motutapu there are the island-top gun emplacements, plus the old barracks in Administration Bay. Stony Batter at the eastern end of Waiheke, accessed from Man of War Bay, has tunnels and gun emplacements open to the public.

Towards a tropical paradise?

As I sit in some Hauraki Gulf winter anchorage, with no boat heating but well wrapped up in fleece clothing, I often wonder why I don't sail offshore, especially to the Pacific Islands, and friends always ask me this question. I've read hundreds of accounts of long-distance recreational sailing. And as part of my former work I've read the tales of the great explorers starting a few hundred years earlier. I'm smitten by them all.

So I do imagine being anchored in a tropical Pacific lagoon, with transparent water full of iridescent fish and rainbow coral, the temperatures in the 30s, and the water temperature the same, and I'm hearing the swish and rattle of coconut palms bending to the trade wind.

Well, would I really want to head off to the Pacific islands (and beyond) in a yacht? Yes and no. The 'yes' bit is easy – it is simply because of emotions to do with adventure and travel and myth long imbedded in me by my culture and my experiences and learning. The 'no' answer is more complicated and based on so many reasons. I don't have the blue-water experience nor a suitable vessel nor the money required to set up offshore readiness and capability. I suppose I could go as a crew with others, if they would have someone inexperienced and past their physical prime.

But there are many other negative reasons. I'm constantly amazed at the frustrations modern off-shore sailors invariably have with bureaucracy, ranging from safety and insurance issues, to customs and immigration and petty corruption, now seemingly everywhere on earth. Plus the difficulties around any necessary yacht servicing and repairs in remoter regions. What the accounts I read make very clear is that as reliance grows on electronic equipment of every conceivable type, so does its unreliability and expense of repair, if such is even possible, rise exponentially. Technology, especially if it doesn't work, can create great anxiety.

And I have serious questions about the fabled yachting destinations, especially in the Pacific. We have travelled through much of Polynesia and Melanesia as part of my university research. We have spent time living in and visiting Pacific communities, starting in the early 1970s. Over 40 years of intensive research into Pacific cultures and history has long since led me to deconstruct notions of the fabled Pacific Paradise – that is but a figment of Western imaginations.[15]

Sure there are physical locations that conform to the idyll, but, like much of the rest of the planet, the Pacific islands are also human landscapes – sites of traditional human brutality, cultural intrusion and conflict, colonial domination, and subsequent social, economic and political exploitation including two world wars, civil wars, military coups, rioting, large-scale corruption, nuclear testing and dumping, pollution and environmental degradation.

It is by no means hell on earth, though you would not have wanted to be in Bougainville in the civil war of the 1990s. Mostly the islands are pleasant enough and in the right spots they can be marvellous, but it is not a pristine terrestrial Paradise. The truth that all is not always well on Pacific islands is shocking to us only because of our centuries-long obsession with the islands as some sort of Garden of Eden.

Pacific islands are no better or worse than anywhere else on the planet, though their very smallness sometimes more readily reveals and personalises the unfortunate side of human existence. Even the quickest visit to a seemingly charming village can reveal things we would rather not see. A travelling yachtie, in particular, necessarily has a personal experience of the authenticities of small island life. There is no escape to private air-conditioned tour buses, flash hotels and exclusive airport lounges to isolate them from what is really there.

But there is another reason for 'no'. Since retiring, Merrilyn and I have journeyed about remote New Guinea and throughout Melanesia, including revisiting some places where we first started our Pacific explorations in the early 1970s. This time we were on a tiny (70-passenger) luxury Australian cruise ship. I was a guest lecturer, giving talks on the history and cultures of the region. In spite of our decades of Pacific experiences as researchers, this was our first taste as typically cosseted tourists.

Most of the days were spent ashore in very remote villages. The ship drew only three metres so could go into atoll lagoons where large cruise ships never had a chance. We even went up the Sepik River. It was all so exciting. Endless variations in language and culture, whales, erupting volcanoes, steamy jungles, crocodiles, canoeing, snorkeling – the whole package, including once hitting a coral reef (fortunately without being holed too seriously). We limped back to a port and got airlifted out.

But we were never quite at ease. We could never forget that we were there with every possible luxury on a ship full of very wealthy passengers, yet we were looking at third-world conditions. Most of the people we saw were eking out a subsistence existence and had, in Western terms, virtually nothing. Yet many of our fellow passengers had brought with them preconceptions of Noble Savages and saw only 'happy go lucky natives'.

We danced and laughed with the locals, and were fed and entertained in their villages. We saw their schools – if they had them. We played frisbees with the kids, and showered them with ice from our cold-drinks chilly bins, and took them on high-speed blasts on our fast landing craft. At one village on the Sepik River there was a tradition that the ship played the locals at soccer – about 40 aside. Can you imagine a large bunch of aging, overweight, retired male passengers (and a few females), running for the first time in perhaps decades on a rough, muddy field pretty much on the equator?

At every departure there were tears. This personal experience was real and genuine. I've never had so many moist-eye occasions in my adult life. In one village in the D'Entrecasteaux Islands off the south-eastern tip of mainland New Guinea, a young girl, Samantha, held Merrilyn's hand all day, and carried her baby brother with the other. We walked for miles with her to see some thermal pools. She gave me a conch which we now have onboard *Mercury*. When we departed there was emotional blubbering. When we returned on subsequent trips we were mobbed by her family and there was more emotional blubbering. I don't normally do that stuff. But it got to me.

What many passengers did not always understand was that these remote people belonged to new nation states (Papua New Guinea, Solomon Islands, Vanuatu) that were quite dysfunctional, with often non-existent or empty schools, little or no medical services, and few opportunities for those that might seek them. Political and community violence is often not far below the surface. Women are often treated very badly, by our standards. The kids have the most beautiful teeth. In their teens many will become addicted to betel nut. Their teeth will go red and rot away, and because they add lime to their betel nut, they have an extremely high incidence of mouth and jaw cancers. Aids is widespread. Every school classroom we visited had walls plastered with aids awareness posters. We saw a few villages stricken with cholera. Life expectancy is about 50.

What I learned from being on the crew side of things was that villages we visited were always checked out well in advance, and also on the spot by a local onboard interpreter who went ashore first. It was exactly like Cook sending ashore Tupaia, his Tahitian guide, to check out the locals. The interpreter for our New Guinea trips, Alex, has become a very good friend.

There were many places in Melanesia where our visit would have been considered a hostile gesture. The cruise company naturally avoided them. And what we saw over the years sailing through these countries was often a marked worsening of their lot, as their governments became more corrupt and unresponsive to their citizens. More schools closing, more malnutrition and more skin infections among the young.

In more affluent centres in the Pacific there are a whole new range of problematic social and economic issues, which is why so many of their citizens choose to live in Australia, New Zealand or the USA. There are more Polynesian people in these countries than in the whole of tropical Polynesia.

There came a point (in 2014) when, after some five or more years, we 'retired' from such cruising, mainly because of the increasing angst we felt, and our growing awareness of our intrusion, no matter how brief or happy, in other peoples' lives.

Whatever their fate, it's their home, not ours. A remote anchorage might be stunningly beautiful, but it's also someone else's cultural space. After over 40 years of experiences in this space, we've concluded that in spite of the rational knowledge we have of the Pacific island world, it is impossible not to come to judgements, no matter how 'liberal', reflecting our own cultural learning and prejudices. We wonder what will become of Samantha.

Of course all our friends think we are mad, giving up our free luxury cruise opportunities in Paradise.

So I'm very happy to cruise the north-east coastline of New Zealand in our old wooden yacht. OK, the climate is not tropical, the water is always cold – but there is no risk of dengue fever, or malaria, or typhoid, or the life-threatening poisoning that can occur from even the tiniest coral cut (which happened to a couple of our cruise-ship passengers). I don't have to worry about customs and immigration and petty corruption. I'm spared the anguish of seeing people whose cultures and lifestyles are getting wrecked. Out of sight, out of mind? Perhaps. But gawking at poverty and subsistence living from a luxury vantage point will not help, and may even hinder.

Mokohinau Islands

Very remote and mysterious, these are the last of the Gulf islands I landed on. A long time ago I knew that they were there, and had spotted their distant, dim presence a couple of times while surfing at Pakiri. But I knew nothing about them until fairly recently when I was a tour guide on a small Australian cruise ship (the same one that took us through New Guinea and Melanesia) that plied an Auckland-Bay of Islands route for several summers.

Landing on the 'Mokes' was one of the highlights. They are not high islands, but small, scattered, rugged and jagged, the worn-down remnants of ancient volcanic upthrusts. Their cliffs have a twisted quality and are streaked with a vivid yellow in many places. Because they're serious reserve islands, landing is permitted only on Burgess Island, where the lighthouse is. The anchorage there, which opens to the south, is dodgy at the best of times, with its boulder sea bed and an invariably heavy ground swell that wraps around from any direction.

Landing is on a boulder beach, followed by a scramble along swampy tracks to higher ground. Then the track veers straight up the steep ridge to the lighthouse, following the now-derelict trolley tracks that enabled supplies to be winched to the keepers' houses and the light. The light is long since automated. There is a large concrete base nearby, foundation for a war-time radar, and a recent A-frame hut for visiting scientists. On a clear day you can see virtually the whole of the Hauraki Gulf.

The three keepers' houses on a sheltered plateau near the top have long been demolished. One of the last keepers, Ray Walter (who went on to be the hero of replanting Tiritiri Matangi Island), begged the Department of Conservation not to burn the last one down, or at least to wait until he had stripped its wonderful kauri timber. He built a launch with it near the top of the island. This was later winched off by helicopter during an air force exercise.

The dry grass of summer is filled with the rustlings of a protected native skink and the squawking of red and yellow-crowned parakeets. The small pohutukawa trees are amongst the most vivid I have seen. The island is mostly grass and scrub due to the wild weather, former burning and also former predations of keepers' goats and cattle. Neighbouring Fanal Island's vegetation has been far less disturbed.

Near the base of the trolley track there are dangerous outlets of numerous volcanic air tunnels hidden in the grass. You only become aware of them when air compressed by large sea swells bursts skyward with an eerie moaning sound. Nearby is a large rocky gut that booms and sprays with the same swells.

Landing, or even a near approach to the islands, is possible only in settled weather and calm conditions. It's not a restful place. The islands collectively do not invite casual recreational sailing given their rugged coastlines and the presence of daunting stacks and half-sunken reefs and rocks. You are very conscious that you're enjoying a temporary stay and that the sooner you're safely out of it the better.

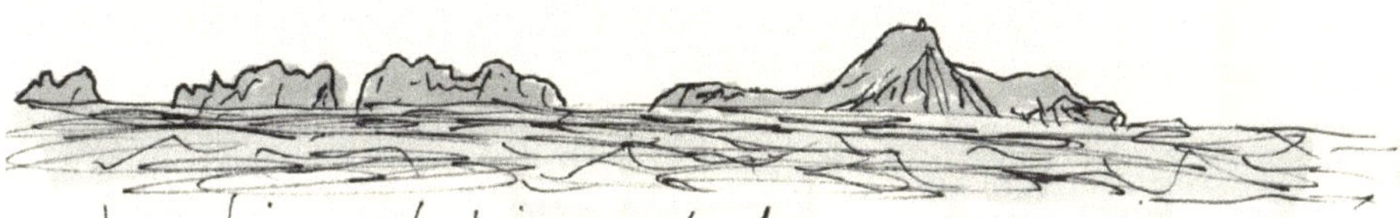

Approaching Mokohinau Islands

I once sailed *Mercury* there from Great Barrier, but I was too scared to anchor in the lee anchorage in a rising wind so I went back. Another time in the yacht we approached the group, also from Great Barrier, but abandoned the attempt five nautical miles out due to very large swells and a chaotic sea, all made worse by the wind suddenly dropping to nothing. Poor *Mercury* slammed and banged about. Even on the cruise ship with its sophisticated landing craft the chances of getting passengers ashore were always only about 50/50.

One can only marvel at how Maori paddled there, presumably waiting long times for settled sea conditions, as we do today. There may have been small and short-lived Maori settlement at times, but freshwater was very limited. Because they're low islands and well offshore, rainfall is low. Certainly Maori were very active visitors on a seasonal basis to catch young grey-faced petrels (northern muttonbirds) and fish. Ngāti Wai are the acknowledged people of the island. The group name Mokohinau is a corruption of Pokohinu (Burgess Island). One translation of Pokohinu is 'an oil-filled recess', referring to the oil of the muttonbirds. Neighbouring Fanal Island is a source of obsidian, which provided ready-made knives for the seabird butchery. Ngāti Wai from Great Barrier Island continued to harvest muttonbirds on Burgess Island well into the 1940s and beyond. One lighthouse keeper noted in 1947:

> *There were about 22 Maoris and about 29 dogs. Livened the place up a bit ... They were a good crowd, really good. They did all their own plucking of the birds and preserving them in their own fat down on the landing.*[16]

Ngāti Wai-Ngāti Rehua still claim traditional rights to harvest muttonbirds on Mokohinau.

The islands still seem to teem with fish in these species-depleted times and attract fishermen and scuba divers in their fast boats. With 30 knots-plus at their command, they are better placed for quick visits than yachties who need to take a much longer-term view of the weather and sea conditions.

Anchoring anthropology

Perhaps the worst feature of sailing in the Hauraki Gulf is overcrowded anchorages during summer holidays. Among the most crammed places are Islington Bay (Rangitoto), Bon Accord Harbour (Kawau), and North Harbour (Ponui). Small anchorages such as Owhanake (Waiheke), Woody and West Bays (Rakino) and bays in Port FitzRoy (Great Barrier Island) can also be gridlocked in high season.

There are defined patterns of group behaviour that for the observer bring amusement, frustration and sometimes annoyance.

It is well known that if you happen to be alone in an anchorage, the next boat along will invariably anchor close to you regardless of often vast empty and perfectly suitable places in the same bay. And once two boats are anchored close to each other any others will simple join the group. It's a herding instinct.

The most desirable spots tend to be closest to a beach and everyone jockeys to be in the shallowest possible water. I'm not sure why. Staying a bit further out will usually give you more room and the sea conditions are likely to be identical. And being close in to a landing spot means everyone and their dog will zoom past in noisy outboard-powered inflatables so the dog can have a crap on the shore.

Once anchorages get crowded, and that can mean well over a hundred boats, finding a spot brings on new patterns of behaviour. There are usually many boaters who are determined to find a place right in the midst of the crowd and will spend ages picking their way annoyingly within a few metres of other boats in their forlorn quest before invariably retreating to somewhere more sensible on the outskirts of the mob.

There are those who can choose a spot to anchor and simply get on and do it. Others anchor, then up-anchor and move on and anchor again, sometimes several times. Then there are those who, having found an anchoring hole in the midst of other boats seem incapable of figuring out that where their anchor is dropped is not where their boat will end up. Down goes the anchor in the centre of the hole, leading to frantic yells from those already anchored as the new aspirant pays out the rode and drifts dangerously close.

This situation is greatly dramatised by the technique of dropping the anchor then slamming the boat into reverse to make the anchor dig in. There is even more trouble in store when, in a crowded anchorage, and in spite of the weather being settled, and there being little or no current, and it's probably only a few metres deep, there's a dogmatic insistence, picked up from some magazine, that the anchor rode should always be ten times the depth of the water, or more. This plays hell with swinging circles and ends up with near collisions and tangled anchor chains.

Daytimes in crowded anchorages can be ruined by kids driving outboard-powered inflatables round and round like great blowflies, causing annoying noise and wake. Wake boarders are worse. Night-time noise in crowded anchorages can also be a curse, ranging from a cacophony of generators running to charge batteries for power-hungry microwaves and televisions, to blaring pop music on the beefiest of stereo systems, and drunk, bellowing males and screaming women.

We avoid crowded anchorages where we can. The best time for yachting is probably autumn, winter and spring, when we are often alone. Above all, we steer well clear of Labour Weekend, Christmas-New Year, Auckland Anniversary and Easter.

North Channel
N
W
E
S
North Cove
smelter
Mayne
Islands
Two House Bay
Bon Accord Harbour
Mansion
House Bay
Mansion House
Kawau Island
Dispute Cove
copper mine
Copper Mine Bay
South Cove
Bostaquet
Bay
Rosario
Channel
Beehive Is.
wreck of
the *Rewa*
Motuketekete
Moturekareka
Motutara
Kawau Region
Motuora

Motutara, Moturekareka and Motuketekete

Motutara literally translates as island of white-fronted terns, or kahawai birds. It is small, scrappy and mainly covered in ancient pines grown large and misshapen. One end is an old stone quarry where a former headland has been levelled right down. A Public Works programme quarried the island from the 1920s to the 1940s. Many of the first roads on the neighbouring mainland and sections of the road to Whangarei were made by gravel from this quarry. There are a few concrete remains of the wharf, including four large concrete piles still standing in the sea which give the wonderful stony anchorage there a certain signature. We often overnight there.

There are still some nice links with that past. The restored scow *Jane Gifford*, which now resides at Warkworth, can often be seen sailing majestically in these waters. She was one of the main carriers of the Motutara quarry gravel to Warkworth and Matakana and elsewhere.

You can walk around most of Motutara quite quickly at low tide, though the foreshore is often quite rugged. The small stretches of 'beach' are all stones. Large stingrays frequently cruise close in. There are masses of wonderfully sweet rock oysters. The bush is largely impenetrable, though in one (secret) place there are some very old loquat trees probably planted by quarry workers. At the right time of the year their delicious yellow fruit hang in masses.

Motutara is completely lacking in any classic island beauty, yet it has a certain charm. It's a pleasant overnight anchorage except in winds from the north. There's also a tiny place to shelter just inside its south-west point. Another favourite spot for overnighting.

The eastern end of the island is joined to neighbouring Moturekareka by a shingle spit, barely covered at high tide. Moturekareka, which literally translates as pleasant or happy island, is a bit larger and is also covered in the same ugly pines. Yet photos taken in the 1920s show little or no vegetation. This island is well known for being the site of one of the best and most accessible sunken ships on the New Zealand coast, the *Rewa,* which lies very close to the shore along one side of a bay which provides a sheltered (and thus often crowded) anchorage.

The *Rewa* started life as the *Alice A. Leigh,* a four-masted steel sailing ship reputed to be one of the largest and most handsome barques of its time, some 90 metres long and weighing 3000 tons. It was built in Cumbria, UK, in 1889 and used extensively on the great sea routes of the age – London to India and Australia, and across the Atlantic and Pacific Oceans. The economics of sail were eventually doomed by steamships. Her last big voyage was in 1922 to Auckland, where she was laid up for many years.

Charles Hanson, veteran of the Boer and First World Wars, who owned and lived on Moturekareka, eventually got the *Rewa* taken there in the mid-1930s. He intended to moor it across his bay as a breakwater, using it as paid accommodation. But the vessel foundered, swung against the shore and sank in shallow water. Early photographs portray the ship still in stately form with decks above water and all four masts standing. Over the years a lot of her gear was stolen or sold. The resourceful Johnny Wray who built his own 11 metre cutter *Ngataki* during the Depression, mainly from scrounged timber around the Gulf, bought some of the *Rewa's* heavy sailcloth to make his own sails, along with other fittings. He immortalised his adventures in one of the great sailing books – *South Sea Vagabonds* (1939). *Ngataki*, recently restored, still sails Auckland's waters, and can often been seen moored in the Viaduct Basin.

A recent nearby find on Moturekareka of a large amount of old, worn, broken glass, very near the site of Charley's house, may be his booze-bottle midden.

The *Rewa* is now reduced to below its gunwales, in parts still several metres above high water. Her masts are long gone, as are her superstructure and decks. Her great outline size still impresses, but more and more of her oyster-covered steel hull is rapidly rotting and crumbling.

Whereas Moturekareka means pleasant island, neighbouring Motuketekete translates as island of regrets. Indeed it is. In the 1840s it was the site of a copper-smelting works, which got its copper in decidedly dubious ways from the main copper seam on Kawau already mined by a rival firm. The island is still in private ownership and quite ruined by being entirely covered in a modern plantation of radiata pines. When I first sea kayaked around it there was wreckage of several boats scattered along its eastern end. Presumably their owners rightly kept the Motuketekete light to port, going north to Kawau, but failed to realise that there's a bit of a reef sticking out, marked by an east cardinal beacon. Doubtless a regretful mistake.

Boat watching

More than any other technological creation, such as a car or an aeroplane, boats represent a several thousand-year tradition of human association. They are thus laden with a heritage that elicits an emotional response in many of us. Whether it is adjusting a sail, tying a knot or keeping a weather eye, it has all been done before, and for thousands of years. Even the simplest, lowliest water craft embodies so much of human cultural evolution. And in an isolated place like New Zealand, everyone until the 1930s had to get here by sea. Even by the 1960s most arrivals still came by boat.

Boats are not just things that float and transport us. They also embody history, culture, dreams, aspirations, nostalgia and longing. A boat is an idea, a feeling, before all else.

And if boats represent so much of our humanity, they can also be a refuge from the more oppressive side of noise, crowding and pollution. Other than tramping in the wilderness, going sailing is about the only other way to create a glorious self-isolation and self-dependence. But sailing is much easier than tramping – you don't have to carry any gear, and the wind moves you effortlessly. A boat can provide a delightful escape. It can be a location of peace and contentment. It can also be a curse if expensive and ongoing maintenance is required, as it usually is. And of course in difficult sailing conditions it can also be a demanding challenge. In fact if you are very unlucky or unwise and/or ignorant, it can injure you or get you drowned.

Every possible type of boat can be seen in the Hauraki Gulf – great container vessels, cruise ships, naval ships, state-of-the-art racing yachts, waka, barges, sailing ships. There are more boats around than you can shake a stick at. Most, though, are pleasure craft.

I tend to put these pleasure or recreational boats into three categories. First, there are the despised craft such as jet skis, together with the huge, several-storeyed fast powerboats that look more like aerodynamic wedding cakes than boats. In crowded anchorages they can be intimidating, especially because with their relatively shallow draft they like to be closest to the shore, and push their way through accordingly. And their anchoring footprint plus their noise both day and night can be a nightmare. Recreational boats just get bigger and bigger. If people want to surround themselves with every home-sized home comfort, why don't they stay home?

The speed at sea of these huge boats is phenomenal, and the wake they generate can be positively dangerous, especially since they will often pass other boats (illegally) within a few metres, presumably because they can't be bothered to tweak the autopilot to divert from their hell-bent course. Or else they are not keeping the required look-out. The massive raw power at a skipper's fingertip is also probably intoxicating. There have been a number of recent instances when they have literally run over small craft. Even if they don't hit you, their violent wakes easily have the capacity to tip people out of cockpits. The only vague consolation for the shell-shocked small-boat crew is the knowledge that these monsters are eating up hundreds of expensive diesel dollars every few minutes.

These wakes travel many miles, and any nice anchorages that they pass at speed are beset with constant washing machine motion. A classic example is Hobbs Beach (Tiritiri Matangi) where countless high-speed power boats hurtle through the Whangaparaoa Passage.

Summer seas are often calmer at night, not just because the wind often drops, but because the massive fibreglass wake generators, like huge jungle creatures, eventually settle down to rest.

Second, there is the large group of nondescript yachts and launches that have few remarkable or unique characteristics. Modern production-yachts and launches tend to dominate this category. They feature lots of boring straight lines and flat surfaces resulting from mass production. They are invariably made of fibreglass, a miracle product but one that is often more functional than aesthetic.

Then, to my eye, there is a third group of boats that is just so appealing. Among them I include non-production, usually wooden, yachts that have a pronounced sheer line and sometimes less common sail-and-mast arrangements, such as a gaff or junk rig. They can range from vintage to modern, but probably the older they are the more pleasing the styling. I love bow sprits and boomkins, and stern-hung rudders, and round portholes. I'm intrigued by bilge keelers that can dry out on the beach. Most vintage/classic craft interest me, as do smaller rather than larger vessels. I also like some of the old wooden commercial-fishing or work boats with high, up-curved bows that have been reinvented as recreational launches. The best example, which is just so perfectly proportioned and shaped, is *Meola,* which we last saw in the Bay of Islands.

But my favourite craft to look at are the launches generically called bridge deckers, especially those built from about the 1910s into the 1930s. These were the pleasure craft of the wealthy that roamed the Gulf in some numbers, right through the heart of the Great Depression. Their design owes something to narrow and shallow-draft river craft, modified for sea use, and they have a good turn of speed. They have a very low, flat, long and simple profile with the most stylish vertical bows. And there are the accoutrements of a past age with wonderful bronze fittings, round portholes and a short mast for a small stabilising sail. They always seem to fly flags. They often have davits. They can have big brass cabin-top air vents. They are proper boats.

In more recent times they have become much respected and valued, often lovingly and expensively restored to former glories. A few years ago a company took off a mold from a 1912 Logan bridge decker and recreated it in fibreglass with a modern interior. About 30 or so modern Logan 33s were built before the company stopped production. We were looking to buy a yacht at the time and had we been rich a Logan 33 might have been a temptation. They really are very pretty.

In my youth I was always building model boats to sail at the beach. My most common design was based on bridge deckers. I sawed a pointed bow, with vertical stem, from a length of '4 by 2' timber, and nailed a long thin piece of wood along most of the top of the hull, complete with round port holes painted in black. Utterly simple and very satisfying to tow about on a piece of string and anchor with a stone in harbours dug in the sand at the beach. I have since made one for each of our grandchildren.

Polynesian boats

The world's first truly ocean-going vessels were developed by Polynesian ancestors in South-east Asia some 4-6000 years ago. Until that time societies in that part of the world had experimented with rafts of various kinds, especially made of bamboo. That was how Australia came to be settled some 60,000 years ago. Later they also started hollowing logs for canoes. But all these craft had obvious limits and could never take people into the vast Pacific Ocean.

The technological breakthrough came when the sail was either independently developed in South-east Asia about 6000 years ago or was introduced at that time possibly from Arab countries. Putting a sail on a narrow hollowed-out log creates an unstable and dangerous craft, but when someone came up with the idea attaching an outrigger to a canoe everything changed. Throughout much of the region canoes were fitted with two outriggers, one on each side, and then with a lateen-type sail. Suddenly humans had the capacity for blue-water sailing.

This outrigger and sail complex was modified and improved all the way across the Pacific Ocean by the Austronesian sailors. In the west, in Melanesia and Micronesia, the exploring vessels were mostly single hull with a single outrigger. Travelling through remote New Guinea I was amazed to see the importance still of such craft, for fishing, for racing and regattas, and especially for long-distance voyaging in the still very vital kula ring trade.

In Polynesia they constructed double-hulled canoes and more efficient sail shapes and it was these highly efficient craft that eventually took them to Hawaii, Easter Island, South America and finally New Zealand.

By the time of European contact, Maori had long since given up oceanic voyaging, and very few dedicated double-hulled vessels remained. Maori canoe technology had instead evolved to suit local conditions, especially rivers and lakes, and so outriggers were generally abandoned. But they were still sometimes used on small coastal fishing canoes, as throughout much of the Pacific, though few if any seem to have survived beyond the 18th century.

Maori also had access to vast trees, notably totara, and also kauri and kahikatea, and so they began building large one-piece vessels. Throughout much of tropical Pacific, certainly east of Fiji, and that means most of tropical Polynesia, there was no large timber so larger vessels were constructed by carefully fitting and tying together many smaller pieces of wood.

Maori canoe building reached its pinnacle with the great war canoes – waka taua – which were both transporters of 100 or more warriors each and also powerful statements of immense mana. Fashioned with ornately carved prows and very tall, carved stern pieces, the largest were 30 metres in length, so long that several dugout trees had to be dovetailed together. The hulls often had wash strakes lashed onto the dugout gunwales along each side to make them more seaworthy. They were extremely large and strong, capable of being dragged over rough portages to lakes and rivers. They were stable at over three metres wide.

Not all waka taua were quite this big, but they were substantial nevertheless and were the main means of transporting warriors.

Often they were paddled at considerable speed. For more stability and greater distance, two were sometimes temporarily lashed close together, so recreating the former double-hulled style, and some were fitted with sprit sails.

Waka taua came to be the scourge of the Hauraki Gulf, bringing several major invasions over the centuries, most notably the Ngā Puhi from the north in early contact times led by Hongi with his terrifying musket-bearing troops.

Even so, coastal sea conditions around New Zealand are often rough and unpredictable and even the largest of canoes were vulnerable in high seas and strong winds. The most fired-up war party would wait for relatively calm weather rather than be swamped. This is why during the early colonial years Maori leaders were often keen to hire or buy or sometimes commandeer the more seaworthy European whaleboats and small sailing ships for trade and travel and sometimes for violent use in their own tribal hostilities.

Rough, windy seas also meant that coastal islands, and notably those in the Hauraki Gulf, were always welcome shelter waypoints. As they are today.

For most day-to-day use, vessels in the Gulf, and elsewhere on the coasts, were waka tete, a single-tree dugout with wash strakes and little if any ornamentation, used for transport and fishing. They are well documented in the descriptions and sketches by early European travellers in the region. Some of the smaller ones had outriggers, but these were very uncommon by contact times. In calm water estuaries and harbours, and on rivers and lakes there were waka tiwai, narrow dugouts without wash strakes and carvings.

Few canoes survived the colonial era, though many were collected for museums here and overseas. Probably every Auckland school child has been taken to the Auckland War Memorial Museum and seen the war canoe on display – *Te Toki a Tāpiri*. It is 25 metres long and was built in the 1830s, and is reputedly the last great waka taua ever used in battle.

Some waka taua have been built in more recent times and are commonly seen on the water during important events such as Waitangi

Day and Auckland Regatta day. And there's been a huge resurgence particularly amongst Maori and Polynesian youth in canoe racing with waka ama – outrigger canoes built in modern materials.

Also in recent decades there has been great interest throughout Polynesia in recreating the great double-hulled voyaging canoes, and these have now criss-crossed much of the Pacific Ocean using traditional navigational techniques. The best known is the *Hokule'a*, based in Hawaii. A prominent New Zealand voyaging vessel, *Te Aurere*, built and based in Northland, is a frequent visitor to Auckland waters. And Te Wānanga o Aotearoa has a replica, *Aotearoa One*, though much modernised, for training its students. It is a common sight in the Gulf.

In 2011 I was sailing from Rakino back to Gulf Harbour and suddenly, against the sunset, there were seven voyaging canoes. It was their first day of a trip out from Auckland that eventually took them to the far reaches of Polynesia – a special moment, an unforgettable sight. It made the mind spin with imaginings.

We carry a large conch shell on the yacht that we were once given in New Guinea. I gave it a mighty blow as one of the canoes swept by, and got a great reaction from the crew.

Captain's log

I have kept a record of all the voyages, even if only of a single day trip, in *Sea Waif*, and then *Mercury*, just noting dates and places. On the longer trips I keep a very rough log in a reporter's notebook which simply notes weather, main activity on sea or land, and any notable events or sights. All this is just for reference, not for any deep reminiscing. I never keep GPS tracks or data such as average speed, time travelled and so on. That always seems so boring and clinical.

One summer I had a new tablet that took remarkably good video clips, before it died just after the guarantee expired. I used a simple computer video editor to put together two to four-minute sequences complete with sound track and sometimes music. I enjoyed the technicalities of doing so rather than the end product itself. I did find it particularly irritating that no matter how rough the sea was it always looked quite calm on the videos. My next, much cheaper, tablet had no such capacity and for that I was grateful. Taking videos could become a chore, as indeed can taking digital photographs, but I still tend to take still photographs of interesting things and views, and I confess to having thousands of images in our computer. I also confess to the recent purchase of a GoPro so I'm back in the video game.

These still and moving images are very seldom shown to other people. They can never adequately capture how we felt and what we thought at the time, so can never really be fully understood by others, and nor should they be. Ultimately all such images are personal. I avoid other people's photographs of their adventures. Our children will never inherit thousands of hard-copy photographs of our sailing since by that time we had gone digital. The digital record will doubtless either be deleted with a mouse click, or chucked out altogether with our extinct technology.

On one *Mercury* trip a few years ago I suddenly started simple sketching. The last time I did this was in 1971 when we lived for a few months in Paris. Why I started again I'm not quite sure, but I think it might have been triggered by hours of watching passing coastlines that reminded me of the coastal profiles sketched on the Cook voyages by Sydney Parkinson and others. So I started doing them too, as well as other scenes, in a small sketchbook, with just a felt-tip pen at first and then I bought a few more pens to add various shades of grey.

My rule is that no sketch should take longer than five minutes, must be done on the spot and can't be tarted up afterwards. They are left raw, so to speak. I found that doing them gave me the most enormous pleasure. I'm not quite sure why. The one occasion I remember most vividly was sailing solo on auto helm into Burgess Island, Mokohinau, with a tail wind. I had only minutes to do the sketch of the island and the lighthouse before having to turn on the motor, just in case, then gybe and tack back out of the lee bay. Very satisfying. Who said that males can't multi-task?

I've filled a couple of sketch books now, and regretfully am running out of Hauraki Gulf subjects. It is the one record I sometimes occasionally look at again. A few of these sketches are scattered throughout this book.

I believe that ultimately the best logbook is in the mind. I've always been a believer in what William Wordsworth said a very long time ago about 'emotion recollected in tranquility'. That is, developing an awareness that having some moving or meaningful experience can be enjoyed at the time, and also in the future. Said that poet:

While here I stand, not only with the sense
Of present pleasure, but with pleasing thoughts
That in this moment there is life and food
For future years.

Little Barrier/Hauturu

Its characteristic shape can be seen from everywhere in the Hauraki Gulf, and it looks much the same from every direction – a series of high volcanic peaks forming a curved skyline and dropping sharply to steep cliffs then into the sea. It is always a deep-blue colour, and often has towering cloud formations above it, or sitting on top of it. Perhaps the most dramatic view of the island is from land rather than from the sea. Cresting the ridge and descending by road into Leigh from Matheson Bay on the mainland, the island suddenly appears, seemingly so close.

Hauturu means resting place of the winds. A poetic name, but also it may be ironic? Given its exposed location, the island indeed can cop the wind from any direction. For Maori it provided areas of cultivable land in some of the lower valleys, and was a major source of seabirds. It was also strategically situated on the sea route between Northland and the well-populated Auckland isthmus. First settlers claimed descent from legendary Toi te Huatahi, then Tainui conquered them and they in turn lost the island to Ngāti Wai – the people colonial government recognised as owners.

Populations probably seldom exceeded about 200. Apart from the usual pa and midden sites, and kumara pits, their extensive gardens feature numerous large terraced stone walls to provide shelter for kumara gardens, particularly on Te Marareroa flat going out to the landing at Titoki Point. Over time Maori cleared some 30 per cent of the original forest cover all around the coastal lower levels.

Today, 'unapproachable' is the best way to describe the island for it is a very serious conservation estate, and has been since the late 19th century. It was recognised early on by New Zealand and visiting overseas naturalists as a potential and necessary haven for fast-disappearing native bird species. Maori had already started running sheep and cattle, but the beginning of kauri timber logging on the island in the 1890s eventually forced the government's hand and it bought the island in 1894 from its claimed Maori owners, who were somewhat reluctant sellers, for use as a sanctuary. Traditional ownership and the sales process is still contested today.

The Department of Conservation keeps almost everyone away, except the few allowed ashore for conservation activities. Being circular, the island affords sailors no safe shelter since strong winds and swells simply wrap right around its rugged, boulder-strewn shores. So it sits there, enchanting, forbidden. But we can read about its treasures, a veritable Noah's ark preserving New Zealand's best range of highly endangered plant, bird and insect species, as well as the endemic reptile tuatara. Introduced predators have been eradicated, namely the Polynesian rat – kiore – brought to New Zealand by Maori and feral cats released early in the colonial period. Cats were eradicated by 1980, and the kiore by 2004.

We had a friend who once got a two-week dream volunteer job on the island, climbing daily the steep rough tracks to replenish bird-feeding stations near the summit. It was all too good to be true for a few days, then in rain and mud it palled, and it ended up a really horrible, physically painful job.

As sailors we do have a navigational use for the island. Sailing to Great Barrier Island from Kawau, we aim at the south-eastern side of Little Barrier to make sure we pass north of the dreaded Horn Rock, before swinging slightly to the right and heading for Port FitzRoy's entrance via Man of War passage. A close pass reveals heavy bush, dramatic ravines leading to the often misty volcanic summits and cliff faces tinged pink. It looks a bit like those old Romantic paintings of New Zealand with their ominous dark bush and rainy mists sweeping over high peaks. Such paintings are usually explained as fanciful European artistic conventions of the time, but perhaps those painters painted what really was there with their sombre, luscious, swirling oils.

A good day at the office

I can get great pleasure from a day at the office – the cabin of *Mercury* moored at Gulf Harbour. There are so many wonderful jobs to do. Among the most pleasurable is routine six-monthly maintenance on the Beta 20 engine.

I start with the cooling system, draining both the fresh and salt-water coolant. Then I remove the impellor cover, pull the old impellor out with long-nose pliers, lubricate the new one with special grease and insert it, and refasten the cover with a new O ring seal.

Then I undo the heat exchanger. I replace the engine anode, and make sure all the numerous tubes in the exchanger are free from any gunk or corrosion. It goes back in with two new O rings. I return or replace the fresh-water coolant, and turn on the seacock for the salt-water coolant.

I next run the engine for a while to check for any water leaks and to warm up the oil before I pump it out. I replace the oil filter, and pour in new oil. Every couple of years I replace the fuel filter, which requires bleeding air from the fuel lines, which is not my favourite job.

Then a check on the gearbox oil (and sometimes replace it), and a final engine test. The grease gun pumps into the nipples on the universal joint, thrust bearing and prop gland shaft.

And before I know it several hours have gone by. Time for lunch of instant noodles made from water boiled in the kettle.

The electrics then get the treatment – battery water levels checked, and anticorrosive spray goes into the several electrical bus boxes I built around the vessel. Interior lights and navigation lights are tested. Battery torches, headlights and spot lights are checked. My home-made water incursion alarm in the bilge, and the manifold heat alarm have their siren shrieks briefly affirmed with their test buttons.

There is always housework to be done – vacuuming with a 12-volt portable unit, wiping surfaces, cleaning the toilet. The diesel tank needs to be kept topped up to help reduce moisture, and the water tank needs to be kept full too. Check the VHF radio and the broadcast radio.

An eye needs to be kept on everyday supplies – toilet paper, detergent, soap, toothpaste, dental floss, tea and coffee, soup packets and noodle cups, salt and pepper, paper towels, methylated spirits for the cooker, and so on.

There is always a list to be made of things that need to be brought on board for next time and other tasks that need to be done.

About time to go home and relax after a satisfyingly busy day.

Tiritiri Matangi

Moby Dick's Ishmael used to head off to sea 'as a simple sailor' whenever he felt 'drizzly November' in his soul. Our equivalent is to head off for a day to Tiritiri Matangi for an uplift of spirit.

The magic begins on approaching the shore because of the birdsong, a fairly unique sound since in most parts of New Zealand the bush is silent. Hobbs Beach is a nice anchorage, providing it is not crowded and there is not too much roll generated by high-speed power boats in the Whangaparaoa Passage. Tui and saddleback are readily visible, flitting about. It's a great place to swim and snorkel off a boat, and sometimes the fishing is good too. We've seen dolphins swoop through the bay, cleaning up mackerel or sprats.

According to Charles Royal, the island's full name, Tiritiri-o-Matangi, literally means 'sanctified heaven of fragrant breezes', a reference to its sacred, mythical Polynesian homeland. But it also means, more prosaically, a windy place, and it certainly is. Listening to Nowcasting, which gives real-time wind speeds and directions,

Tiritiri Matangi very often has the highest recorded wind gusts in the inner Gulf.

Tiritiri Matangi was originally settled by Kawerau Maori who built a pa on the hill at the northern end of Hobbs Beach. Ngāti Pāoa later built a rival pa, Papakura, in the north-western headland. Kawerau destroyed Papakura pa about 1700 but both tribal groups continued to use the island. One of the island's attractions, apart from its strategic and gardening possibilities, was fishing, snapper of course, but also small spotted sharks which were caught in large numbers and sun dried for storage.

An archaeological investigation of a small area near the wharf indicates human activity by the 1400s, and evidence in middens of fish and bird remains, even of moa (obviously brought from elsewhere). There was also some obsidian from Great Barrier and Mayor Island, all indicating small, mobile Gulf communities, travelling widely, collecting and perhaps exchanging commodities. Later on more permanent settlements appear on the island.[17]

The island was abandoned in the 1820s during the raids from the north by Hongi and his musket-armed Ngā Puhi warriors. Some Kawerau families returned in the 1830s but seem to have had a short-lived presence on the island. With the construction of the lighthouse the Crown's assumed ownership of the island, as part of its Mahurangi Purchase of 1841, was confirmed. The island was leasehold farmed until 1970.

Maori cleared a lot of the original forest cover of the island, burning it for garden space and to stimulate the growth of bracken fern that was beaten into an edible paste. More bush clearing to run sheep and cattle in early colonial times soon left a barren landscape. There's a remarkable 1883 painting by Alfred Sharpe looking at the island from the sea off the south-western corner. Entitled 'A grey day off Tiri Tiri', it captures the sheer rocky cliff faces, the scruffy treeless landscape and the towering lighthouse. The sea is typically choppy, the sky a high overcast and dreary, perhaps the last stages of an anticyclone with rain not far away. There are boats busily going about their business – a dinghy, yachts and a couple of steamers. We sometimes fish on this very spot.

Yet Tiritiri Matangi is now known internationally as an island restored to something as close as possible to its pre-human state. The remarkable story has been told often, and most notably by Anne Rimmer in *Tiritiri Matangi. A model of conservation.* In brief, the island came under the control of the Hauraki Gulf Maritime Park Board in 1971, at a time when a few natural scientists were pushing for it to be replanted and turned into a predator-free sanctuary for endangered native birds and insects. The now barren island was at times overrun by kiore. Farming was stopped. A bold plan was eventually devised, driven in particular by John Craig and Neil Mitchell, to use volunteer labour for mass tree planting and for the island always to have public access. It's been a great success. Kiore were poisoned, a nursery was built on the island to propagate local seeds, between 1984 and 1994 almost 300,000 trees were planted by enthusiastic volunteers and native species were introduced.

The island's modern godfather is Ray Walter, who lost his lighthouse-keeping job when the light was automated in 1984 and became instead chief nurseryman and general leader of the restoration project, always supported by dedicated island enthusiasts. The citizenry of Auckland has genuinely embraced the island literally as a treasure. Some 35,000 people are permitted to visit on the commercial ferry each year (150 per day) plus anyone else who can get there in kayaks and boats. There is now a wonderful Ray and Barbara Walter Visitor Centre, full of maps, photographs, models and displays and well known to Auckland school children.

The stunning success of restoring Tiritiri Matangi set the precedent for similar restorations on Motuora, Motuihe and Motutapu and elsewhere, including fenced-off parts of the mainland notably at Tawharanui, the end of the Omaha sand spit, and the end of the Whangaparaoa Peninsula.

Going ashore at Tiritiri Matangi there is a maze of tracks through the now-maturing bush, along the hill tops and out to headlands and beaches. It's probably the best place in New Zealand to see native birds, I think better than Motuara Island in Queen Charlotte Sound and Ulva Island at Stewart Island.

All around there are tui, bellbird, saddleback, stitchbird, North Island robin, fantail, whitehead, fern bird, tomtit, red-crowned parakeet, and sometimes kokako to name the main ones. Kick at the leaf-covered ground and North Island robin will descend and peck at minute insects. Several bird-watering stations attract large numbers of birds, especially stitchbirds, saddlebacks and bellbirds. At night you can hear kiwi. The highly endangered takahe casually wander anywhere, but most often on Hobbs Beach and near the lighthouse. Takahe were thought to be extinct but some were found in remote Fiordland in the 1940s. A careful breeding programme in captivity has seen their numbers rise slowly to about 300 – but they are still one of the world's most endangered bird species.

Tiritiri Matangi is called an open sanctuary because the public are free to wander anywhere. It's been a bold experiment to enable such ready access to a place of highly endangered species. Most people who visit the island, and thousands do, show great respect. Though we are sometimes disturbed to see the occasional boatie take a dog ashore for a crap. Poison stations and traps are constantly monitored for predators that might come ashore with boating parties.

One day we spied a dead, very bloated animal body on Hobbs Beach. I thought it was a pig but on closer inspection it had a long tail and was a wallaby. We told the Department of Conservation staff who probably thought we were deranged but they went to have a look. The wallaby had drifted from Kawau where they live. It was promptly removed.

The main tracks can sometimes get a bit busy, and the incessant chatter from some people can detract from the bird-watching experience. But off the main tracks we can generally be alone, especially wandering towards the north end of the island.

One favourite walk is to head up to the ridge from the northern end of Hobbs Beach and out to the site of the ill-fated Papakura pa on the northern tip of the island, also the site of the wartime radar. There are great views of the Mahurangi region. Sometimes we go down to North-east Bay with its craggy rock formations. Back along the ridge that follows the island's spine to the lighthouse and the Visitor Centre with its dinky nature shop and educational displays. If there's time we take the Wattle Track back to the wharf and along the shore to Hobbs Beach, passing the penguin nesting boxes.

We return to the mainland usually feeling at peace with the world. Restoring an island helps to restore us all. Above all, it provides a ray of hope in an otherwise environmentally fraught planet.

Weather watch

The Hauraki Gulf seems to have more weather than elsewhere. Maybe it's because there are so many weather forecasts and observations available. There are detailed VHF forecasts separately for the Waitemata Harbour, the Hauraki Gulf and from Bream Head to Cape Colville. There is also the marvellous Nowcasting (on VHF and also on a phone/tablet app), which gives average and peak wind speeds and direction for Bean Rock, Tamaki Strait, Tiritiri Matangi Island, Mokohinau, and Channel Island. The web provides more weather information than you can digest – wind maps, isobar maps, rain maps, rain radar, satellite images, swell heights and so on. The ready availability of smart phones and tablets makes all this information instantly accessible on coastal seas.

Yet it does have some limits regarding forecast accuracy. Mostly it's reliable for the next 24 hours but after that it can be a moveable feast given the changing nature of the weather. Expect four seasons in a day, they say. The one area where forecasts are now fortunately quite accurate is picking up tropical cyclones far to the north, giving several days warning. But locally generated weather bombs can sometimes catch forecasters unaware.

In the good old days of youth I remember, probably very inaccurately, what seemed to be a simple weather pattern. For most of the time the winds blew from the south-west bringing fine weather in summer and rain and showers in winter. For the remainder of the time they came from the north-east or east which in summer could bring fine weather or rain and storms, and in winter mostly bad weather. There were only very brief north/north-west and south/south-east periods as the winds veered and backed around the compass. If you want proof of this wind pattern look at how all the airport runways around Auckland are oriented north-east/south-west.

But this simple wind pattern, if it ever existed, apparently no longer does. We now know that major seasonal wind directions have to do with the broader Pacific water temperature zones which create El Nino, or La Nina weather systems. These two take turns at influencing the New Zealand weather for a few years at a time, and they can lock winds into prevailing directions for months, or not.

And this overlays the more day-to-day weather behaviour with the endless progression of high and low-pressure systems, which generally travel across the Tasman Sea from the west.

So it's all rather complex. My rule of thumb is that there will always be either a head wind, or no wind, or too much wind from any direction. This should mean that I am never disappointed. But of course I am. Expecting the worst does not preclude hoping like hell for the best and being dismayed when the worst happens.

Also there's my rule which says changes can be almost instantaneous, for example transition from a glass-like sea state to a 20-knot steep chop in minutes, or changes might take many days or even a week or so. In moments of optimism I figure that if bad weather can suddenly occur, so can good weather. When I'm in pessimistic mode, bad weather seems likely to hang around for a long time.

I'm a weather-forecast addict and access vast amounts of information. Merrilyn just looks out the window. What she sees is what we get.

There is a distant connection between the Hauraki Gulf and the beginnings of modern weather forecasting. Robert FitzRoy, after whom Port FitzRoy on Great Barrier Island is named, was an officer in the Royal Navy. He is best known for his captaincy on the voyage of the *Beagle* which had Charles Darwin on board, and of course he was also the second governor of New Zealand, after Hobson.

Less well known is the fact that FitzRoy was the first to start systematic recording of weather to try to delineate patterns and so offer the first weather forecasts – a term he invented. He also carried out various experiments measuring changes in air pressure and relating them to weather conditions. He organised a system of storm warnings around the British coasts. FitzRoy has belatedly been recognised as the founding father of the British meteorological office, and in 2002 the UK marine weather forecast area Finisterre was renamed FitzRoy, the only UK marine forecast area to have a person's name.

I always think of FitzRoy when I give the barometer a tap. Everything is connected to everything else.

My preferred wind is from the south-west at about 12-15 knots, which makes sailing the Gulf in most directions quite easy, and there's plenty of available shelter for overnight anchoring. The only route not good in a south-westerly is coming back from Great Barrier. The worst wind is anything from the east/south-east which seems to kick up a very short, sharp and uncomfortable chop and makes for rather too many lee shores for safe anchoring.

The characteristic and uncomfortable Hauraki Gulf chop is largely due to the shallow Gulf waters. But there is something strange about the sea state in a south-easterly. When I was young a neighbour who worked for the Auckland Harbour Board once knew a proper diver, one with lead boots and a great brass head piece with a port-hole window and a pipe to the surface for air. One tale the neighbour relayed to me was that while working underwater almost anywhere in the Gulf it is possible to tell when a south-easterly is about to spring up because the water at the bottom suddenly goes very dark. No work is possible so it's time to head for the surface and not come back until the wind and weather changes.

There is also the common phenomenon of a strong wind against tide, especially in narrower passages. The Whangaparaoa Passage and Motuihe Channel can be positively dangerous in these conditions with two-metre-plus waves so close together that even a relatively small boat can have its hull bucking on two of them at the same time. And around Great Barrier Island and in the Colville Channel sometimes there can be some very nasty tidal rips and overfalls.

But in relatively good weather the Hauraki Gulf provides some of the best cruising grounds in the world, and I know this to be true because Peter Blake once said this to Phil Smallfield who sold us *Sea Waif*.

Maori, and all other pre-industrial maritime people, were acute observers of the sea state and weather and saw things few modern citizens ever bother to notice. In this they were more like European sailors before modern forecasting began – attuned to their environment rather than to some electronic box.

Maori sense of changes in the weather and seasonal weather patterns evolved from a good understanding of weather phenomena. They noted cloud shape and colour and movement, and water vapour ringing the sun, and the movement and behaviour of certain birds. The seasons were accurately calculated by changing sun rising and setting points on the horizon and daytime sun angles and especially movements of certain stars. We are now all familiar with Matariki, when the Pleiades first rise above the north-eastern horizon at dawn about early June signalling the new season and the time to prepare the ground for kumara planting.

Growth stages of plants and trees also indicated seasonal change, as did the departure and arrival of migrating birds.

I like to imagine that Maori forecasts of old were at least as good as ours of today. They observed and interpreted what they could see. Like Merrilyn, they looked outside.

Hen and Chickens

These are the most interestingly named islands in the Hauraki Gulf. Cook mostly gave obvious or boring names to so many places, yet every now and then he came up with something whimsical, even inspired (such as the Aldermen Islands and the Poor Knights). Once you know that this group is called the Hen and Chickens there is no other way to see them but as a guardian hen and a whole line of her bustling chickens. The Hen is a high volcanic island, which features a peak of craggy volcanic towers forming a coxcomb. The Chickens are low and small, and have sedimentary origins.

Anyone travelling north by road and crossing the Brynderwyn summit will be familiar with these dramatic island shapes out in Bream Bay, complimented by the equally striking volcanic peaks of Bream Head and Mt Manaia at the entrance to the Whangarei Harbour. It's one of the great New Zealand views.

Most boaties never get very close to the Hen and Chickens, except for high-speed recreational fishers and divers. They are islands that most people just sail past on the well-worn seaway from Cape Rodney to Tutukaka and beyond. That route takes you just to the west of the Hen, and virtually slap bang into neighbouring Sail Rock, a lone sentinel of a volcanic stack that takes on weird shadows and sinister shapes as you pass close by. We usually sail between Sail Rock and the Hen. Going north, and looking up to the right, there's a great view of the 'balancing rock' on the Hen's ridge line – a thin volcanic pillar seemingly with a precariously balanced overhanging topknot. From some angles it looks like a fat cross.

For Maori from the wider Whangarei region, especially Ngāti Wai, the Hen and Chickens (the Hen called Taranga and the Chickens collectively known as Marotere) provided a bountiful fishing and muttonbirding resource.

There are 67 recorded archaeological sites on the Chicken Islands, including some nine pa sites, terracing for habitations, some stone walls, storage pits and middens. But it is thought that any actual settlement was likely to have been small, perhaps no more than 50, and not necessarily permanent over any great length of time. These islands were more likely visited on a seasonal basis, and may have been a place for occasional refuge.

Hen Island features a range of larger archaeological sites with more extensive stone terracing, walls, mounds, rock shelters, storage pits and middens. The extent of the stone work is notable, much of it associated with gardening. There was certainly much more gardening activity than on the Chickens, and it is therefore likely that a larger and more permanent resident population could have been supported, perhaps numbering up to 100. The middens contain many shells from the mainland, suggesting close two-way contact with local mainland communities.[18]

As a result of tribal fighting during early European contact times the islands were abandoned.

Joel Samuel Polack claimed ownership of the island group in 1845 but Governor Grey disallowed the claim and leased it instead to Isaak Merrick, who was involved in copper mining on Great Barrier and Kawau and manganese mining on Waiheke. Merrick dug some shafts on Coppermine Island, the easternmost in the Chickens group, and sent some 20 tons of copper ore to Auckland in 1849. He then shipped it to England but no subsequent record of it exists.

There was no further mining interest until 1899 when a company was formed to reinvestigate the copper deposits but that came to nothing.

The Australian company Conzinc Rio Tinto carried out soil analysis and test drilling in the period 1965-69 but concluded that any copper deposits were uneconomic to mine. Thank goodness.[19]

As quite isolated and relatively unmodified islands, the Hen and Chickens were home to many species endangered on the mainland, though some of the islands were affected by fires from camping fishermen in the 1880s. But overall the islands were early recognised nationally and internationally as having special conservation significance due to rare flora and fauna.

As with the Poor Knights and Little Barrier there was much interest in the tuatara. By the early 19th century Hen Island was the only place in New Zealand, and the world, still to have saddleback birds.

The islands were purchased by the government in 1883, and declared nature reserves in 1925. Kiore were removed from most Chicken Islands in the 1990s and from Hen Island in 2011. However, for cultural reasons to do with Ngāti Wai's claimed guardianship of kiore, the Department of Conservation has left them undisturbed on Mauitaha and Arāra Islands in the western Chickens group. Unlike other rat species, kiore cannot swim. So they are stuck where they are and can't recolonise the rest of the Hen and Chickens.

The Hen and Chickens are now very serious conservation islands. No landing is permitted anywhere. A large range of endangered insects, reptiles and birds have been translocated to there (and saddlebacks *from* there to elsewhere) and the island group now rivals Little Barrier for its conservation significance. It's another Noah's ark.

City viewing

There are stunning views of downtown Auckland from around the inner Gulf, especially looking back into the harbour from around Motuihe and Browns Island/Motukorea. But its beauty is best appreciated from such a distance rather than actually being in the CBD with its choked roads, crammed footpaths and rubbish blowing along its windy canyons. Sailing on a sparkling sea is not only attractive in itself but it also means that you are not somewhere less pleasant, such as in the CBD.

There's an irony in that there are two obvious things about distant cityscapes that you are often less aware of on land – noise and air pollution. The city seems to me to get louder, or I am more conscious of its noise, as I head into quieter, watery spaces. You need to be well beyond Rangitoto or Motuihe before the low frequency rumble of a million cars finally disappears. Those of us who live in Auckland unconsciously learn to screen out much of this background racket. Arriving at a place like Motuora or Great Barrier Island makes me very aware of silence. I can hear it.

And on days with little wind a low-level brown pall hangs above the city and its suburbs. We pride ourselves that we don't have the dreadful levels of pollution of the larger overseas cities, but that's mostly because we have a very windy climate.

Further out in the Gulf the high points of the city skyline stand out – the volcanic cones, the Auckland and North Shore hospital buildings, and the Sky Tower. The latter is still readily visible from Kawau.

Further out again the city sinks below the horizon, leaving only the summit of Rangitoto popping up. From this distance the city's presence is still obvious from overflying aircraft, especially if they leave vapour trails. And at night there's the bright loom of the city's lights across the southern horizon.

Even out there the city's presence is notably obvious with the rubbish of its good citizens blown offshore by the south-westerly – beach balls in summer, plastic drink bottles, plastic bags, plastic containers of all kinds and so on. Much of this rubbish lands on the shores of inner Gulf islands, and much goes beyond.

We've been on a couple of organised beach cleanups on Rangitoto. The volume of rubbish lying about is shameful.

The fish and I

Like many Aucklanders of my generation, I fished from an early age off rocks at North Shore beaches, at the sewer tunnel discharge pipes at North Head and off the Devonport wharf.

My parents were keen fishers. They netted sprats at Narrow Neck beach for bait, usually having to release most of them back into the water because there were so many, then went fishing in the Rangitoto channel. Those were the days when you could literally catch a boatload. Black and white 1950s family photos show what now seems an embarrassingly large array of snapper ritually laid out on a canvas sheet on our backyard – sometimes 30 or 40 of them. They fed the neighbourhood.

My post-war generation experienced in its youth the very last stages of the Hauraki Gulf marine bounty, and even then it was probably a pale shadow of what it once had been. But there were still large snapper, tarakihi, trevally, kahawai and bait fish there for the taking.

We readily caught crayfish in pots or by just snorkeling in shallow water. There were paua, oysters and mussels everywhere. The seabed was covered in sea eggs – for those who acquired the taste. The tidal bays were full of pipi, tuatua, cockles. There were still large beds of scallops. But that was before we all went mad in the modern world.

My dad was a basic hand-line man, though he also embraced the new technique of surf casting, starting with a homemade Rangoon cane rod with a side-caster reel. He was an early experimenter with a wind-powered kontiki to drag a line with numerous hooks out to sea. His creation was a car inner tube with a mast and a square sail that dropped when a barley sugar sweet dissolved in the water. At the same time the sinker fell and took the hooks down to the bottom. To get it out a really long way he discovered that peppermint sweets took longer to dissolve. That contraption must have caught hundreds of fish over the years. One occasion I vividly remember was when we went to Port Jackson at the end of the Coromandel Peninsula (which was a daunting car journey in those days). He set the thing off with a good offshore breeze only to have it stop suddenly not far from shore. Thinking that it had got snagged he cursed for a while then struggled to haul it back. The line had got caught alright – by eight massive snapper.

Whenever I see today's fishing kontiki with their sleek, plastic, semi-submerged shark profile, the battery-powered propeller and retrieval reel, and the fully automated GPS guidance system, costing $5000 or more, I smile inwardly. The next generation of kontikis will be radio-controlled drones. Not a smiling matter.

My other fishing role model was Alan, an old family friend in Northland. Sitting in Alan's old dinghy fishing, dad and I would listen to his many wondrous tales, often about his wartime adventures with the Maori Battalion in Italy. One that left its mark was when the troops got hold of some black market purple-coloured vino. There was shock and horror when many of them immediately vomited up great long purple tape worms that none of them knew that they had in their guts.

But suddenly he would go quiet, and get really hunched in his bow seat, and his whole demeanour would change. He would close his eyes. It was as if he were listening for fish. Then he would start catching them, always far more than anybody else in the boat. I once asked him how he did it and he replied that he 'thought like a fish', telling me that he pictured his bait gently moving in front of him, so he knew when it would be hit.

My dad and his mates always used hand lines when fishing from a boat. Once my dad hooked onto a massive kingfish. He spent 40 minutes or more before he got it up to the boat, then he and his two companions struggled to get it onboard where it created mayhem in the tiny 3.6 metre clinker dinghy. His hands were a bruised and cut mess. There was blood everywhere.

He had dreamed of catching a kingie all his life so he was very proud. 'It's an ambition realised,' he said, and the tale and that saying became legendary in the wider family. There remains a faded Kodachrome 35mm slide of him holding it. It was almost as long as he was tall.

My parents gave me a marvellous fishing rod as a lad, made of a short, stiff piece of 'green heart'. My earliest triumph with it was landing a 4.5kg (a classic 10-pounder) snapper from the Devonport wharf, earning a photograph in a local paper. I still have the beloved rod, and the photograph.

My 1950s fishing tuition has left me with a preference for fishing basics. I'm not impressed with the bewildering array of flashy gear in fishing shops, although I always have a look just in case there's something that I might find useful. I don't like the current fashion for long, whippy rods, especially when fishing off boats. No matter how small the fish these rods always spectacularly bend double. I prefer short and fairly stiff rods. But I do use a whippy soft-bait rod and Asian sabiki hooks for catching mackerel.

I've tried fashionable soft baits, with all the proper gear, but have now reverted to type – like my dad I'm a bait man, and my usual rig is a sinker on the bottom and two very short traces above it, but with 'modern' circle hooks.

We have a fish finder built into the yacht's GPS sonar option. We mainly use the sonar for checking anchoring depths. As a fish finder, it tells awful lies. I've caught fish when it says there are none there, and not caught them when it beeps and goes crazy with fish symbols. I don't bother with it now while fishing.

When sailing I always drag a lure. I've stopped running this from a rod because pirouetting about the transom in a choppy sea while fighting a big kahawai, or in my dreams a kingfish, is probably not the smartest thing to do, especially if sailing solo. So now I have a 30kg line on a big plastic hand spool and I haul any catch in, hand over hand, fairly quickly and brutally.

To avoid bird strike, especially when dragging through flocks of squabbling terns, petrels and shearwaters, I now use only diving lures – ones that go down about three metres.

Using simple gear, I like to think that I catch as many fish as anyone else, and probably more than many. Day fishing in the Whangaparaoa channel usually enables me to provide fish for the neighbours, though with the daily legal limit of seven snapper they don't get a lot. When away cruising on our yacht, with no fridge, we are content with enough for a single feed.

My range of fish caught in the Hauraki Gulf is predictable. Mostly kahawai, a few skipjack tuna and one kingfish on the lure. Mostly snapper, with a few gurnard, John dory, trevally and the like with bottom bait. My favourite fishing spot is anywhere in the Hauraki Gulf where I last caught decent fish.

Maori fishing – full circle[20]

Polynesian people were amongst the world's most efficient catchers of fish, given their oceanic environment and the significance of seafood in their diet. Those that came to New Zealand brought their fishing practices with them, adapting them to some new materials and some different fish. Along with their tools and weapons of war, their fishing technology dominates the archaeological record that is displayed in museums throughout New Zealand.

Maori had a huge range of fishing technology and tactics that rivals anything most recreational fishermen have these days, plus a few extra tricks. There was no species that they could not catch, except whales. Sharks and dolphins were harpooned. Small game fish such as skipjack tuna, barracouta, kingfish and kahawai were taken on lures, other fish on hooks and in nets and traps.

There were many styles of exquisitely made trolling lures and fishhooks. One key characteristic of Maori fishing gear, and indeed of most aspects of their material culture, is the effort that went into not only making a functional fishhook (or tool or weapon) but into also decorating it with symbolic shapes and markings. These go well beyond the purely decorative, indicating the significance that these items have within the wider spiritual world. It's a true blend of function with belief.

Early European depictions of Maori fishhooks are sometimes in themselves beautiful works of art, especially those created by draughtsman Sydney Parkinson on Cook's first voyage.

Lures were made of bone, wood and sometimes coloured stone such as serpentine or greenstone. Lacking tropical pearl shell, Maori often inlaid lure bodies with paua. Lure tips, sometimes barbed, were usually made of shell or bone.

Hooks for line fishing were typically made of one or two pieces of bone, shell or wood, or a combination of these materials. Often they did not have barbs. Unlike modern metal hooks they were not usually designed to penetrate into the fish's flesh, but most had a characteristic recurve shape, or what we now call a circle profile, that rotates and locks inside the fish's jaw. Our recent 'discovery' of the effectiveness of circle hooks, which are now all the rage, is very many centuries behind Polynesian fishermen.

When Maori first saw metal fishhooks they immediately appreciated the value of that material, but not the J shape of the traditional western hook. Maori sometimes rebent them into the circle shape and filed off the barbs.

But during the contact period Maori soon mostly gave up making their traditional fishhooks – eventually it proved much easier and quicker to trade or buy ready-made metal ones. And to some extent fishing itself sometimes became a little less important in their diet given the introduction of the European potato, other vegetables and pigs. Not only were the new foodstuffs produced for their own consumption but they produced surpluses to sell in the new colonial market.

Pre-contact archaeological sites in the Hauraki Gulf and region reveal a plethora of hooks and lures, yet it may be that most of the fish caught in the Gulf, and elsewhere, were netted. Because nets were made of vegetable fibre they have not survived well in the archaeological record, unlike hooks. When Cook sailed about the Firth of Thames he noted a large number of stakes or posts used for supporting nets all along the shallower shores.

The nets could be huge. Cook saw some up to10 metres deep and a kilometre long. This amounts to industrial-scale fishing, and indeed snapper bone and scales in middens show a decline in size over time suggesting a reduction of numbers. Serious spotted shark fishing with nets in places like Kawau Bay must also have had an impact on stocks. Early European travellers recorded thousands of them at a time being sun-dried on frames. A large bio-mass of mackerel and other school fish such as maomao and mullet was also taken in nets. There were also hand scoop nets and large hoop nets lowered to the bottom then raised around an unsuspecting school of fish.

There were fish traps of various kinds. There were round pots made mainly of supplejack, very much like modern crayfish pots, for trapping crayfish and Moray eels.

Large areas in shallow, tidal bays were surrounded with long stone walls to trap fish once the tide went out – another technique brought from tropical Polynesia. Examples of these are readily seen at Colville Bay and Browns Island.

Maori also exploited what must then have been vast resources of shellfish in estuaries and coastal places. The whole of the Hauraki Gulf was a giant marine food basket.

They were highly technically proficient in catching and gathering marine resources. Cook commented that none of his men were a match for Maori catching fish, and in spite of our modern technology including fish-finding sonar, I think that they were probably better fishermen than most of us today.

One can still sometimes learn something from old Maori fishermen. Their traditional fishing calendar was more attuned to what was actually happening in the sea and when, and obviously did not have to take into account weekend or holiday fishing priorities. Many modern 'Maori fishing calendars' and 'bite time' predictions, now commonly built into GPS and available as apps, are just commercial hocus pocus.

There is not much recreational fishing technology that we have today that did not have a Maori equivalent. But they also used a few tricks seldom seen now, such as banging bags of rocks on the rocky sea floor to entice groper, or knocking canoe floors with stones to attract sharks. Another neat trick allowed them to get a line and hooks to float free on the bottom in deep water without being tethered by a sinker. Any old stone was bound with flax, or similar, with about 30cm of leaf protruding. The baited hook point was inserted into the leaf close to the stone and everything let go overboard. When the stone hit the bottom the hook was given a few sharp tugs to tear it up through the leaf and then the hooks drifted naturally on the seabed. The people in remoter parts of Melanesia still use this technique.

Of course Maori fishing was a necessity, not a recreational activity in itself, though it was obviously also a social occasion. And it was steeped in fishing lore of great antiquity and significance. Every fish in the sea was the child of Tangaroa, the sea god. And after all, what we prosaically call the North Island was Te Ika a Maui, the fish of Maui. His magic hook was made from his grandmother's jawbone.

Tender behind

With *Mercury* we inherited a neat little fibreglass dinghy moulded like a wooden clinker one. It was good and stable but oh so heavy. I attached retractable plastic wheels but they were mostly of no benefit. Almost everywhere we went ashore the sand was too soft, or the beach was shingle, or mud, all of which made wheels worse than useless. Two of us struggled to carry it.

One winter I decided to build a lightweight tender that we could readily carry up a beach. I found free internet plans for a darling little thing called Apple Pie. These were based on a 1930s version, modernised for plywood, stitch and tape construction. It is two and a half metres long, flat nosed, and consists of only five plywood hull panels – a bottom, two sides and two ends. Fortunately there is an excellent website by Christine de Merchant with instructions and many photographs of her day-by-day building progress.

I had always wanted to build a wooden boat. So I spent a happy winter month or so building my Apple Pie in the garage, taking photos every day. It was my first serious experience with stitching the edges with wire, mixing and applying epoxy resin glues and fillings, and applying fibreglass cloth. The basic hull construction was easy. Attaching gunwales and seats and fitting out was much more time consuming. I loved doing it, though the wood, glues, resins and paints eventually cost a small fortune. The cost of ever building anything larger would be prohibitive. And I now fully understand why any individually built boat simply cannot be price competitive with one that is mass produced.

Launch day and sea trials at a local beach were very exciting. To my delight she floated to her lines and rowed straight and true from the centre seat with one person on board, as well as from the front seat with a second person on the rear seat. It also towed true behind *Mercury*, mainly, I like to think, because I built an oversize keel. She will only ever be rowed. Carrying an outboard and fuel is too much hassle on our yacht.

She has proved easy to carry by two people (even by one).

Then came the naming. Candidates were *Tender Behind* and *Love Me Tender*, but the winner was *Transit of Mercury*, which not only relates to our yacht's name but associates with my hero Captain James Cook and his astronomical feats.

There is some downside. Merrilyn and I are small people and (touch wood) still agile. We can easily get on/off *Transit* at *Mercury's* stern and we find the dinghy stable even in rough chop. But a few of our larger and less agile friends have a challenge.

Transit also has a bottom which is quite curved from stern to bow. At the bow the bottom emerges a few centimetres off the sea. At anchor when there is a slight ripple or small chop, the waves bang up underneath the raised bottom. At night the dinghy can get quite noisy as it slaps and chuckles. Various supposed solutions have not worked. Putting weights on the bow seat overnight or hauling the whole thing out of the water alongside *Mercury* on a halyard have proved to be a pain.

One problem, in common with many tenders, is that they love to bump and nuzzle the mother ship when anchored, especially at night. With virtually no mass below the water line, dinghies don't always lie the same way as a yacht in slight current or wind. *Transit* now has a small homemade drogue clipped to her painter at her bow. This has been a great solution. Mostly it works. The trick is to remember to unclip it before heading off in the morning.

Tender travels

Transit of Mercury is mostly used to get us ashore from where we might be anchored. But we sometimes use it for close inshore exploring. Not being outboard powered, it does not travel any great distance, but we like pottering closely around coastlines and inlets and even when rowed slowly it can cover a reasonable amount of ground, or sea.

Favourite little routes, and routines, include circumnavigating tiny Motutara, cutting inside the dinosaur-backboned rocks to the south and crossing the shallow shingle spit joining Motutara and Moturekareka on the high tide. You can usually see the bottom and darting fish all the way around. During their breeding season the nesting gulls and terns can create an aggressive racket.

The two tidal reaches at the end of North Cove, Kawau, are fun to explore. Even at high tide the water is still very shallow. On hot summer days there are often numerous stingrays resting or circling in the warmth, and schools of mullet and sprats dozing until they get frightened and crazily spin off. Normally you can't see these fish themselves because they are so well camouflaged, but it's their shadow on the shallow bottom that gives them away. The inlets take you past baches hidden in the kanuka, and tiny jetties, and dinghies in various stages of repair hauled up along the shoreline. Often the human habitation seems delightfully run down, yet comfortable. Eventually the oars scrape the bottom and it's time to turn and drift back with the floating leaves on the slowly ebbing tide.

These two little estuaries are comfortable, sleepy places, yet something is always changing thanks to the endless tidal ebb and flow.

There are two streams in Port FitzRoy suitable for dinghy exploration. The Kaiarara stream has numerous shallow entrances, many chocked with tree stumps and branches washed down from the steep slopes of Mt Hobson. But having found a suitable entrance it's possible to travel a short distance firstly through low-lying marshlands then overhanging bush. The river bed and banks consist entirely of worn boulders, again from off Mt Hobson. Apart from the trinkling of the freshwater stream when above tidal level it's very quiet and still. It is hard to imagine the old times when hundreds of giant kauri logs came thundering downstream under the pressure of water released from the kauri dams. We would not survive for a nano-second.

The Wairahi stream can be dinghy navigated for quite some distance. There are longstanding tales of how some locals who live hidden on its banks are very hostile to any nosy travellers, some intruders even given warning shots across their bows. It's a good tale but rather a bit stretched. It was the home for a 1970s and 80s hippy commune, but is gentrified now. The few people we have seen always give a cheery wave, though in some of the heavily wooded regions we saw a few individuals slide back into the shadows as we went along. It's probably a very private community, and one very privileged to be able to live in splendid isolation with only sea and river access. Rowdy, nuisance-making visitors may rightly not be welcome.

These FitzRoy streams have high-tide-only access and both require some investigation to find the best entrance channel.

Birds - at sea

So many of New Zealand's seabirds can no longer breed on the mainland due to human-introduced pests. Many species now exist only on offshore islands. The Hauraki Gulf is a major location for these survivors. It is also a destination for visiting birds from the very extremities of the Pacific Ocean. Seabird life is prolific, though overall in decline.

My favourite seabird has always been the Australasian gannet. Large, elegant and graceful, it can wheel about the sky for ages without flapping its wings, looking much like a Concord with its beak angled downwards to assist its vision as it scans the sea far below for likely prey. Then a lightning dive from a great height at almost terminal velocity, a last-second folding of the wings, an almost splashless entry, a wicked set of underwater manoeuvres, then surfacing with a fish to be gulped down. Their soaring elegance belies their ruthless and efficient killing capacity. But of course all birds are brutal. They kill to eat. As we do.

Occasionally there are gannet-feeding frenzies when dozens will dive on prey in a fairly small spot. Sometimes this has happened very close to our boat. You can see them several metres down, literally flying underwater. Apparently they have the odd accident as they smash into each other and they sometimes try to take another bird's catch – all while underwater.[21]

Gannets breed in colonies. In the Gulf there is one on Gannet Rock, just off the north-eastern tip of Waiheke, some on the islets of the Motukawao group near the Coromandel Peninsula, others in the Mokohinau Islands, and in the Broken Islands of Great Barrier. The Department of Conservation has just started a new colony on Motuora Island having recently attracted some breeding pairs with decoy birds and amplified recorded gannet-colony chatter. Rotoroa Island is also starting a colony.

One of the main colonies in the wider region is on Auckland's west coast, at Muriwai, where the public can have spectacular close-up views of nest building, courtship and chick raising. A high point is to witness the dramatic moment when the fledged young birds make their first flight – a remarkable non-stop journey to south-eastern Australia. There they remain for two to three years before returning to Auckland to begin their own breeding cycle, often mating for life. They can live for over 30 years.

My saddest day sailing in the Gulf was when a gannet dived on my trailing kahawai lure off Tiritiri Matangi and somehow got hooked in the wing. I have never known gannets to do this before. It was perhaps old and going blind? It could not fly but kept wildly thrashing about on and under the water. There was no way I could get it near the boat and I had no alternative but to cut the line. I sailed away and heard its plaintive, doomed cries for a very long time. Its friends keep wheeling above it.

I have never seen any albatrosses in the Gulf, nor, as far as I know, any of the large mollymawks. But both can be present.

My second favourite local seabird is the black petrel, somber and dignified, like a black cross in the sky. They are endemic and nest in holes near the top of Mt Hobson on Great Barrier Island, and high on Little Barrier. They have the ungainly and seemingly dangerous habit when landing of crashing through the forest canopy and literally falling on the steep, stony ground to get to their burrows. The reason that the Department of Conservation has constructed thousands of wooden steps on the three tracks near the summit of Mt Hobson is to protect their breeding places from human feet. Alas their numbers are in steady decline, mainly due to them taking baited hooks on commercial long lines now found right across the Pacific Ocean. Black petrels annually migrate to the tropical Pacific and South America.

The grey-faced petrel, or northern muttonbird, is also a Gulf breeder, and historically significant for Maori. Southern Maori prized the sooty shearwater, or the southern muttonbird.

There is a bewildering range of petrels throughout the Gulf that breed on various offshore islands. Some are annual visitors from far away. Identifying the many different types is a task for the experts, and well beyond me. I can identify but a handful, and at any distance they all look much the same.

Then there are the shearwaters, almost as varied and more numerous than the petrels. Most common are Buller's shearwaters, which breed only on the Poor Knights Islands, and which can readily be identified by an M-shaped pattern across their upper wings (or a W shape depending on whether you are looking from the front or the back). Then there are the smaller sooty shearwaters and fluttering shearwaters. All these birds can spend hours skimming the waves around a boat. At times, when it is calm, the fluttering shearwaters land and form a vast carpet on the sea.

Both petrels and shearwaters breed in holes and burrows on the offshore islands. Both adopt the bush crash-landing technique when going to their underground nests. And both can travel prodigious distances. The sooty shearwater and Buller's shearwater, for example, range far to forage food for their young; and after breeding they fly to far-north Pacific regions or to the Americas, before a return to New Zealand for the next breeding cycle. The sooty shearwater is an amazing diver, typically to depths of 16 metres or more. The grey-faced petrel ranges several thousand kilometres offshore for food during its breeding time, and between breeding seasons it heads off to Australia and the north Tasman region.

Also common at sea are the ever-busy white-fronted terns, or kahawai birds, so useful for fishermen in locating boil-ups of small anchovie-type fish that are chased in turn by kahawai, snapper, kingfish and sometimes dolphins. They always look so smug when lined up on rocks, always facing in the same direction, with their shiny black flat-topped heads – like 1950s Brylcreamed bodgie boys. The larger Caspian terns have red bills and are less common.

Seabird activity seems most intense on choppy, windy days. It's as if the wind and sea stir up small particles of life upon which they feed. Flat calm seas often, though not always, see a marked absence of seabird life.

And everywhere there are the delightful little blue penguins that swim far from their land burrows each morning and return at night. A boat can get quite close to them before they dive. They might typically make 800 dives for food a day. On shore at night they often create a great racket with their squabbling.

Then there are the nasty bully boys of the sea – the Arctic skuas that migrate here each summer. It is common to see them harry and have spectacular aerial dogfights with kahawai birds that have caught small fish in their beaks. Inevitably the kahawai bird has to drop the prized morsel – and the skua invariably catches it before it falls into the sea. How dare these foreigners travel all this way to behave like this.

Though I'm very much a book-learning person, I found most of the standard reference books on New Zealand seabirds (and other birds) that might be in a boat library are mostly unsatisfactory in that the authors are obsessed with taxonomy, or the minute identifying of vast numbers of varieties of birds. Whereas the more I learn of these details (and then forget) the more I feel that there is a whole dimension to bird watching that gets skant attention – the social life and behaviour of birds. However, one good recent source on these matters is New Zealand Birds Online.[22]

Seabirds have the most varied and resourceful adaptations to their world. There are those that lay eggs on bare ground, and those that go far inland to breed in burrows and caves. Some are marvellous swimmers and divers. Many seabirds fly many thousands of kilometres on a seasonal basis. Some never leave the locality. Some are solitary, others are gregarious.

I find it awe inspiring that some small feathered scrap of life flying around our boat can have such amazing physical capacities and almost unbelievable migratory lifestyles. The more I see the less I know and understand of seabird life, and the more fascinating, and humbling, I find it.

Birds – near the shore

In anchorages and on the shore there is a whole new range of birds to observe, apart from the ever-present gulls. My favourite shore bird is the lugubrious oystercatcher (again there are several varieties), dark with red eyes and a long red bill. They seem ungainly, even comical. Their chicks are amazing grey balls of fluff perched high on long legs. I always associate oystercatchers and their haunting calls with the beach at Motuora where I first had extended contact with them.

Then there are the active New Zealand dotterels motoring along beaches with their high-speed, staccato steps. They are supposedly endangered, but we nevertheless see them on beaches all over the region. In addition there are various plovers, and wading birds such as stilts.

My least favourite bird is the shag (again several varieties), mainly because it roosts in numbers in pohutukawa trees and slowly kills them with droppings. In recent years they have also taken to pestering me fishing off our yacht, diving down after baits, seizing snapper caught on lines, and catching and swallowing whole any undersized snapper that are thrown overboard. In other cultures tethered shags/cormorants were used by fishermen. A neck ring stopped the shag from swallowing the fish. I'd sometimes like to wring their necks.

Herons, both reef and white faced, I find similarly unpleasing with their snake-like necks and long, looping flying style.

On the borders of sea and land, and especially in estuaries around the Gulf, there is a plethora of birds best seen from the land rather than from boats. The vast tidal flats near Miranda in the Thames estuary are internationally renowned for their huge numbers of godwits, plovers, sandpipers, turnstones, curlews, knots and stints – all summer visitors from the Arctic. Even right outside our house on the Orewa estuary there is an annual summer flock of bar-tailed godwits. They fly non-stop from Alaska just to see us. Tracking devices show that they cross the Pacific at about 3000 metres on the way to New Zealand in about seven days. They return to breed in Alaska via a stopover in Japan, or China or Korea.

Birds – Maori knowledge

Maori understanding of birds was obviously not based on science, yet in some ways it is just as insightful, even more so. Through acute observation they identified all the species and varieties, and named most of them after the calls they made. They knew where and when they were to be found and understood their breeding cycles and habits generally. They were well aware, for example, that visiting godwits did not breed here, and had a pithy saying that when something was impossible to achieve it was akin to looking for a godwit's nest.

They divided the bird world into two broad categories – birds of the land and birds of the sea. These in turn were divided into birds that lived here all the time, manu Maori, and birds that visited from overseas, manu tawhiti.

Birds were a fundamental economic resource. Until they were wiped out, moa were a major source of food, as were larger birds such as kaka and wood pigeons. But the most prolific birds available were seabirds, their chicks and their eggs. What we now call muttonbirding was widespread throughout New Zealand, including the Hauraki Gulf. In northern regions of New Zealand they were mostly grey-faced petrels (northern muttonbirds), which breed during the winter, and their chicks were captured in November. In southern New Zealand they were sooty shearwaters, and they were taken in May. The practice continues there to this day, under Maori control.

Young chicks were hauled out of burrows during the day, or, when the chicks were old enough to leave their shelter at night, they were rounded up in large numbers. They were killed quickly. Their stomachs were pressed to make them regurgitate precious stomach oil that was used for medicinal purposes, colouring and preserving. They were plucked, their heads, wings and feet were cut off, and the torso stored in fat in gourds. In southern New Zealand where gourds did not grow they were commonly wrapped in split bull kelp. I tried some commercially available muttonbirds when I was young. I remember an overpowering stringy, fishy, salty taste.

Bird feathers were woven into cloaks and other clothing, and decorated the hair and body, weapons and tools. They were also used as insulation. Certain feathers were prized more than others, such as those from kokako, two types of cuckoo, gannet, kingfisher, and the now-extinct huia. Red is a sacred colour throughout Polynesia, and the red feathers of kaka were valued. Bird bones were used as needles and in fishhooks. Skins were used in clothing, body decoration and making little perfumed sachets worn around the neck.

Maori had considerable interest in flight. Their mythology often features flying men. They were also great kite makers, usually in the stylised shape of birds.

A whole range of bird-catching techniques developed – from bird spears, to snares, nets, water trough attractors, even to imitating their noises.

Maori bird lore, so well described by Murdoch Riley in his book with that title, gives insights into the pervasive mythological role that birds played in everyday Maori thought. Birds were messengers of the gods and of ancestors, they were signs of supernatural will, and they were daily symbols and omens. Their habits were used to predict the weather, or success or failure in war.

Every bird had its story, its explanation. For example, saddlebacks and stitchbirds were with Maui when he beat up the sun to make it slow down in the sky. These two birds were supposed to bring water to the triumphant but exhausted Maui after his fight. They didn't, so Maui angrily threw them against the sun lying crumpled on the ground. Maui's hands, still hot from his fight, burned the brown back marking on the saddleback; the stitchbird got its yellow marks from falling against the sun.

Birds also had their own great historical events. At one time there was a major war between the land birds and seabirds. Shags had apparently set it off because they were arguing amongst themselves as to whether they were land or seabirds, and the squabble spread and eventually engulfed the whole bird world.

This is as good an explanation as any for most human warfare. And it's another good reason why I don't like shags.

In fact I also have another reason which again comes from one of a number of Maori sayings about the shag's rigid head and neck in its fast, level flight – in this case the bird is likened to a self-important person hell bent on a mission. In my university life, we applied this imagery to certain individuals who, with their ties tightly knotted, were always striding most purposefully to some important meeting.

Birds – their fate

New Zealand, above all else, was a land of birds before human arrival. With no land mammals, apart from a bat, birds had no enemies except sometimes other birds. And, according to evolutionary processes, birds with no predators on islands tend towards ground dwelling, non-flying and gigantism. And so we had some of the biggest birds ever with moa, and lots of non-flying birds like the takahe and kiwi, along with many birds that could fly but spent a lot of time on the forest floor and often nested on the ground.

New Zealand in these distant times was largely covered in podocarp forest and the country was a chorus of birdsong. Now, in what little remains of mainland bush, there is silence.

As the Maori population grew, so did their impact on the new land. Some 160,000 moa were wiped out in less than 120 years, as were seal colonies in the northern North Island, and snapper in the South Island. Snapper in the northern North Island significantly decreased in size over time, according to their average scale size measured in middens.

Birds perhaps suffered the most since many were non-flying or ground inhabiting, or ground nesting. Dogs and, especially, kiore, did major damage eating eggs and birds. Kiore also decimated snails and lizards and other insects, and browsed a range of new plant growth. Seabirds were harvested annually in vast numbers.

Forest cover was reduced by 40 per cent overall in New Zealand by Maori, mainly through burning. That too had major consequences for birds.

Between first Maori settlement and European arrival there were over 30 bird extinctions.

All these generalised developments took place on even small islands. In the Hauraki Gulf the kiore and the dog ran rampant, reducing bird populations. Maori also cleared original forests for gardening. Islands such as Waiheke, Tiritiri Matangi, Motutapu, Rakino, Browns Island and Kawau, as well as much of the Tamaki isthmus, were reduced mostly to open scrublands. That further hurt both seabird and land bird populations. Only on the larger islands such as the two Barriers and high in the Coromandel ranges was bird life less affected because forest cover was never completely destroyed.

Maori were no better or worse than any other human communities when first entering uninhabited places and rapaciously exploiting resources. It is what all humans do.

With colonial settlement things got much worse for birds. Another 20 or so bird species became extinct. A vast number of introduced predators, such as ferrets, stoats, weasels, Norway and ship rats, mice, dogs and cats wrought havoc. And the clearance of most of the rest of the original forest cover for timber and farming, plus the introduction of foliage-ravishing possums, sealed the fate of many native bird species on the New Zealand mainlands. Their only refuge was on some offshore islands, and then it was still tenuous.

In more recent decades the Department of Conservation, together with various supporting groups, has done a remarkable job in making many of these islands, many of them in the Hauraki Gulf, predator free and replanting native bush. By carefully managing a breeding and translocation programme, many species of land birds (and insects) have been saved from certain extinction, as least in the meantime.

Which is a key reason why the islands of the Hauraki Gulf are so special, not just to Auckland, but to the whole of New Zealand, to the international scientific world and to humanity. Islands such as Little Barrier, Tiritiri Matangi, Cuvier, Motuora, Motutapu, Motuihe and Rangitoto have become vital lifeboats for birds. And the predator fencing of neighbouring peninsulas at Whangaparaoa, Tawharanui, and the sand spit at Omaha is finally encouraging some native species back to the mainland. There are also a number of smaller predator-fenced locations, some built by the Department of Conservation, others by private individuals.

These places, and this work, have a significance that can sometimes seem little appreciated by the population at large.

And the sad fact is that even the surviving species of both land and seabirds are greatly reduced in numbers, most continue to decline in numbers, and many are listed as endangered. Those most at risk are dependent on the continued human provision of predator-free locations and breeding and translocation programmes.

Motuora

If I have a favourite small island in the Gulf, it is probably Motuora. I came across it when I first joined a sea-kayaking network in the 1990s, paddling from Sullivan's Bay in the Mahurangi. The island, with its crystal-clear waters, shining white beach and noisy oystercatchers, together with the small beachside campground, all seemed perfect and made an enormous impression on me. Merrilyn and I have since kayaked there very many times, camped, explored and loved every minute of it, both summer and winter.

As regular campers we got to know the Department of Conservation rangers well, and a good sea-kayaking friend of ours, Clive Hookham, sometimes acted as a temporary ranger. The highlight of one visit while he was there was to score a helicopter ride as it lifted two huge new plastic tanks from the campground to near the top of the island.

To Maori, Motuora was known in several ways. The literal meaning is island of wellbeing. It was also seen as an anchor because it looks like an anchor stone with a hole in one end – Motuora has a tunnel through its south-western tip. Another interpretation is that Motuora was a canoe that was towed but became grounded where it now is – the tow point is that tunnel.

From the main beach you look over the Mahurangi coast and

the doubled humped mountain, Tamahunga, and over to Motutara, Moturekareka and Motuketekete. The beach faces north-west so there are usually stunning sunsets. From our tent door we have seen dolphins swim past, giant stingrays cruising by in the shallows with their wingtips flicking well above the surface, and endless boil-ups of bait fish attacked by kahawai.

In the evening blue penguins waddle ashore and noisily squabble and fight in their burrows at both ends of the beach. Kiwi screech throughout the night. We have sometimes gone up the bush tracks to try to spot them, but without success. We also sometimes make a night trek to the island's summit to see the distant glow of Auckland's lights and the winking navigation lights of the Gulf.

When I started sea kayaking to Motuora it was a paradise for sea kayakers. They were almost its only visitors, and motorised arrivals were not common. Alas in peak summer season and on fine weekends it has now become a very crowded place. I once counted over 40 fizz boats either anchored or annoyingly tethered to the shore with long lines across the sand to high-water mark. But at other times of the year, as with so many Gulf islands, you can be pretty much alone.

We still go there on our yacht, usually mid-week, anchor off the beach, swim in the clear water, walk the tracks, gaze over the Gulf from the lookouts, and take much pleasure in seeing the island's amazing and very rapid transformation.

For some inexplicable reason Motuora has always been predator free, but it was farmed and reduced mostly to grasslands and scrub. George Grey bought the island in 1863, the year after he bought Kawau. He leased out Motuora over the years but came back every shooting season. Because it was a predator-free island, quail were plentiful targets.

The picture-perfect Still Bay, on the south-eastern side, was the secret site for an illicit alcohol still before and during WWII – hence its name.

After a long succession of owners who struggled to farm the island it was fortunately purchased by the Crown in 1965 and in the mid-1990s the Department of Conservation and the Motuora Restoration Society started a tree-planting programme. As on Tiritiri Matangi, many local seeds were propagated on the island in a nursery and planted by a large number of volunteers. Within a few years the planting programme was completed and the island is now almost covered in rapidly growing native bush.

It is satisfying to return to an area that we helped to replant on a number of planting expeditions – in most cases now we can't get to the exact spot so flourishing and dense is the tree growth.

Motuora is a kiwi nursery. Young chicks are released and recaptured when they are old enough to better fend for themselves and then re-released on the mainland. The island has also become the home of a range of introduced species including the giant weta, shore skink, and Duvaucels gecko. Pycroft's petrel, the northern diving petrel and whitehead have also been moved there from other islands in the Gulf to start breeding colonies.

The Department of Conservation has recently successfully started a gannet colony on the eastern headland. For several years would-be breeding birds were enticed by decoy gannets and recorded gannet speak blared out over the sea. In 2014 there were 12 breeding pairs.

It is a great place for recreation, but more significantly it is a place where so much natural restorative good is being done by good people. Visiting Motuora is a perfect antidote to the modern rushing world and its possession-obsessed citizenry. On Motuora other more basic things matter. Indeed an island of wellbeing.

Lighthouses and lights

Many of my generation in childhood dreamed of being a lighthouse keeper. There was something seemingly so romantic in the lifestyle – an exciting place to live, sleeping in a little round bedroom, safe from booming seas and raging gales, and far away from the crowded world. And all you had to do was turn the light on at dusk and off at dawn and give the glass lenses a bit of a polish. Then, as we got older, there were tales of keepers maintaining a kindly watch and sometimes saving mariners in trouble, and providing accurate weather forecasts.

In truth, life was often hard for keepers and their families. Yet something was lost when New Zealand lighthouses were automated in the 1980s. As befits our contemporary world, yet another worthwhile tradition, real or imagined, was suddenly ended. At the very least there are those who say that marine weather forecasting is now less accurate than when keepers looked out their windows and regularly radioed weather observations.

There were only ever a few manned lighthouses in the Hauraki Gulf – Tiritiri Matangi, Mokohinau, Cuvier and Bean Rock.

Bean Rock is an Auckland icon right at the Waitemata harbour entrance. It is a wonderful hexagonal house with a 360-degree verandah, set on a lattice work of supports. It could come from a child's story book. It was manned only in the 19th century and very early in the 20th, and then by a single keeper. He lived in Devonport and rowed out for each night's work. The lighthouse is so attractive to look at by day. At night its light always seems rather disappointing because it is hard to see amidst the glare and glow of a million Auckland city lights.

The other common symbol of Auckland is the striking red and white 'lighthouse' tower on Rangitoto's western side; yet it is not a lighthouse but a port beacon, flashing a single red light every 12 seconds. It was never manned, nor ever intended to be.

Tiritiri Matangi is the most easily seen lighthouse at night for Auckland residents and those sailing the Gulf, winking away every 15 seconds. It was a two-keeper station. During WWII it was a naval station. In 1956 it became the brightest light in the southern hemisphere thanks to Sir Ernest Davis, who paid for a new 11 million-candle power light, but it has since been depowered. It is the oldest working light in New Zealand, shipped out from the UK as a cast-iron kitset in 1864. Its tower is beautifully proportioned, shiny white (though it has been red for much of its history), with a bright-red door, and its place of origin is proudly cast into its side – Pimlico London. Rumpole would be pleased.

Yet for an island with a light working as early as 1865 there were a remarkable number of shipwrecks around its immediate coastline. The cutter *Marwell* foundered on (probably) Bollon's Rock in 1870 while racing, the skipper allegedly drunk. SS *Triumph* ran into the rocks directly under the lighthouse in 1883. No lives were lost. The European officers were quickly taken off the island, but the Chinese crew remained for a month or more camped on the beach – now called Chinaman Bay. That a steamship should run aground within shouting distance of a lighthouse caused great amazement in Auckland, and a few canny boat owners took out paying sightseers. The fully rigged barque *Royal Tar* went under after hitting Shearer Rock in 1901. Divers can still see some of its remains.

Mokohinau lighthouse on Burgess Island is a rather squat, round tower, but it is topped with a large, pleasingly shaped glass dome. Two-thirds of the tower was built in concrete and the remaining section, the light room, was constructed of quarried stone blocks that were shipped to the island.

The light began working in 1883. It flashes every 10 seconds. Being so remote it was a three-keeper station. The climb to it from the landing is up a steep ridge, along the ruins of a small tramway that was built to haul supplies. I've led many a panting cruise ship tour party up that track.

There's a laconic description by one keeper of the day the trolley got loose at the top: 'The trolley took off. You can imagine, it's on a 45-degree angle and … she's really roaring when it hit the bottom. So being a carpenter I had the job of rebuilding this thing.'[23]

The light was turned off during WWII to prevent German raiders getting a fix; coast watchers were stationed there and a radar tower built. Not too far from Mokohinau the bullion-laden vessel *Niagara* was sunk by a German mine in 1940. A coastal cargo boat, *Puriri*, requisitioned by the navy to search for more mines, hit one itself and sank not far from Bream Head. Not until 1947 did the keepers return and the light start up again.

The other formerly manned lighthouse, another three-keeper station, is remote Cuvier Island on the far-eastern fringes of the Gulf. This was built in cast-iron pieces made in Auckland and hauled directly up the steep cliff face. It first shone in 1889. The keepers' houses were near sea level and there was a difficult zigzag track to get them up to the light. It has a 15-second flash. Like Mokohinau, the light was turned off during WWII and it became a radar station. Relatively few Hauraki Gulf sailors have been there. It is off the beaten track, and there is no public access as it is now a predator-free island and is used as a sanctuary for endangered native birds, especially the saddleback.

The glass lenses from the original Cuvier light have had a remarkable history. When the light was modernised in 1982 the massive lenses, weighing several tonnes, eventually, after a long story, ended up in a Department of Conservation shed at a forestry fire station in the Pureora forest, in the central North Island – of all places. There they languished for 15 years. In November 2014 they finally ended up on display at the Ray and Barbara Walter Visitor Centre on Tiritiri Matangi Island, another long story. It is hoped eventually to house the now-reassembled lenses in a lighthouse museum under construction in an adjacent building at the foot of the Tiritiri Matangi lighthouse.

Life on both Mokohinau and Cuvier was tough. Records from both islands feature endless complaints about isolation and privation. Supply ships that were scheduled for every three or four months were often unable to get near because of stormy seas, and mail and supplies were sometimes cut off for six months or more.

There is a lovely story about Mokohinau's keepers in 1908. Desperate for supplies they resorted to building a tiny tin boat with tin sails and put letters inside pleading for assistance. The tin vessel made it to the mainland and supplies arrived just over a week later. Their unlikely mail boat is in the Auckland War Memorial Museum.

Lights like Mokohinau and Cuvier with their three resident keepers – a head keeper and first and second assistant, plus their families, each in their own separate wooden houses – always ran the risk of social tension if one family felt excluded. Married men were always preferred, presumably to avoid any sexual jealousy, and in practice wives were valuable extra (and unpaid) hands.

I've always loved lighthouses, and still do. I've built model lighthouses for each of the grandchildren with an electronic circuit that ramps an LED up to peak brightness then fades, simulating the revolving lens of the real thing.

If there are few actual lighthouses in the Hauraki Gulf, there are myriad navigation lights. There are white flashing lights in many strategic island and coastal mainland locations. Some have red sectors indicating danger zones. Then there are large numbers of lit port and starboard beacons and cardinal and isolated danger marks. The full light list for the Hauraki Gulf in the *Nautical Almanac* is many pages long.

I have often wondered why there are some lights not too far apart which have the same flash times. For example, Mokohinau and Taranga both have 10 seconds, as do Tutukaka and the Cavalli Islands further north.

Mariners are very well served by lights in the Hauraki Gulf. There are many sailors who take the well-worn route from Auckland to Kawau at night. They pick up the Rangitoto port beacon, then head for the light on Tiritiri Matangi, keeping it to starboard with the Wellington Head light on the Whangaparaoa tip to port. Then across to Motuketekete with its light to port, lining up on the white sector of Martello Rock, and passing between the cardinal lights on Motuketekete and Passage Reef. After Martello to port it's a starboard turn into Bon Accord Harbour. All very satisfying, if you get it right.

Lights can be great comforters, winking away in the dark; and like so much to do with boating, they are steeped in myth and tradition. You are never quite alone at night.

The Noisies

The Noisies form a tiny archipelago consisting of two main islands, Motuhoropapa and Otata, the sinister islet Orarapa (it looks like a skull), plus the scattered, reef-choked Ahaaha and David Rocks, and Maria Island.

With regard to these last three places, Merrilyn on a Day Skipper course with Ted Chapelle was told in no uncertain terms 'Just don't go there!' So we don't, but we do visit the two main islands, though mostly Otata.

The Noisies have always intrigued me, especially when I learned that there was such a place beyond Rangitoto. But not until my sea-kayaking days did I visit them, and I did so regularly in illegal camping forays in the off season. That's when I discovered so many of my now-highly-secret places for mussels. The oysters are not bad either. I also explored the outlying reef systems, quite safely in my sea kayak since it draws only a few centimetres. But sailing anything with a keel near them is certainly asking for big trouble.

The very name Noisies intrigues me too. One common suggestion is that it came from some French explorer, who called them noisettes, or hazelnuts, because they looked like a scattering of them (and they do), and the word has since been corrupted to Noisies – now pronounced Noizies to keep some sort of French twang. The only obvious candidate was Dumont d'Urville. But when I read his journal to confirm the story I discovered that he never mentions them and his chart records only the Maori name, Otata, so the mystery remains. The spelling of the islands' name is inconsistent. They are commonly spelt Noises, and this is what appears on modern marine charts. A computer trawl in Papers Past gives their first newspaper appearance as Noisies, in 1879, and that spelling continued thereafter. But by the early 20th century they also appeared as Noises. I prefer Noisies since that is what I grew up with.

The islands are notable for their intricate rocky coastlines and marvellous bush cover, in contrast to their grassy neighbours, Rakino and Motutapu. Vegetation on the Noisies has always been the least disturbed of any of the inner Gulf islands, and was how all these islands might have looked a very long time ago. Pohutukawa trees glow like embers in early summer. It's a really pleasant place to spend a day cruising, fishing, swimming, snorkeling and just hanging about. They are as unspoiled as any Gulf islands can be, though their waterways are pretty busy in the high season. Fizz boat owners in large numbers commonly drag scallop dredges endlessly up and down a circuit just off the main Otata beach.

The islands have been owned by the Neureuter family since 1933. Their wonderful little cottage is nestled in the bush. The owners and their friends seem to be there over summer, but at other times the place is deserted. The bird song is a delight, and has improved markedly since Norway rats were exterminated in 2002. But it's always been a great place for seabirds especially, probably because the surrounding seas are rich with marine life on the extensive reefs.

Noisies birdlife has been long studied by ornithologists, helped by its bush cover and proximity to Auckland. A historical survey from the 1930s to the 1980s lists the presence of 52 bird species – 20 seabirds and 32 land birds.[24] Another study in 2004-06, some years after the Norway rats were eradicated, shows an increase in bird species breeding on the islands, rather than simply visiting.[25]

In my view one of the most stupid rat-related experiments took place on the Noisies in 2005. Having got rid of Norway rats in 2002, the Department of Conservation and the University of Auckland deliberately released a male Norway rat complete with radio transmitter on Motohoropapa. The point of the experiment, it was claimed, was to test methods of rat detection and elimination.

Well, Mr Norway Rat was monitored for four weeks as he successfully avoided traps, baits and rat-sniffer dogs. After 10 weeks the radio signal stopped and the rat disappeared. It was finally detected when its droppings were found on neighbouring Otata Island, where it eventually took a fresh penguin bait in a trap. It had been on the loose for 18 weeks.

The experiment, it was defensively claimed, has 'significant implications for efforts to keep islands free of invading rodents for conservation purposes'.[26]

It certainly does. It seems that the main implication is that if you let a rat loose on an island you may never find it again. Most of us could have told the researchers that before they started their little game.

Another strange animal escape involved the Noisies. Jin, the Auckland Zoo's short-clawed Asian otter, escaped from her enclosure in 2006. She slithered down the zoo creek to the sea and spent 26 days on the loose, being spotted in the Waitemata Harbour, off North Shore beaches and off Rangitoto. She was eventually found holed up in a cave on Motuhoropapa at the Noisies and successfully trapped, using a bait cunningly mixed with her own poo. She was then deported to Wellington Zoo.

The act of sailing

Leaving aside the obvious attractions of recreational sailing – the nice destinations, balmy summer evening anchorages, fishing, exploring in the tender or ashore, swimming, lazing about, socialising and so on – what is the appeal of the actual act of sailing? Yes, there is that magic silent moment when the engine gets turned off, the sails fill, the boat heels slightly and water starts chuckling past at a good clip. But what fills in the many hours that there may be before the next destination?

For me it's all about a sense of immediacy, of the here and now, everything is of the moment. How I sailed in the past or might sail in the future is irrelevant. My opinions about the state of the world are of absolutely no consequence. There is now a task to be done. That is to sail as well as I can and hopefully arrive at some intended destination. So I always keep a good lookout, for other vessels, for hazards, for changing sea and wind conditions (and for whales, sharks, dolphins and birds). I love watching the sky and the passing coastlines and islands.

I listen for unusual creaks or bangs or groans. I've sometimes been driven mad by rhythmic bangings that I feel through my feet as much as hear, and the culprits, after much frustrating searching, have turned out to be things like a breadboard swinging on a bulkhead, a utensil sliding about in a drawer, ball sinkers rolling in a tackle box. I once heard a faint squawk-like sound every time the autohelm adjusted the wheel. I sprayed CRC like a demented pest controller into every possible site of friction, to no avail. Later, on an anchorage, I fiddled around with the steering box and found a couple of grub screws holding the wheel shaft that could be tightened a turn. I was rather relieved.

I like to feel the boat's progress. Is it sailing smoothly or is something vibrating, or otherwise not quite right? A sudden decrease in speed might mean something is caught on the keel or rudder, seaweed perhaps, or a sheet of plastic. There's plenty of both in the Hauraki Gulf.

Then there are the complex workings of the sails, such as adjusting the size of the genoa with the furler, or tweaking genoa sheets, or the genoa sheet cars, or the mainsheet, or the vang, or the mainsail outhaul. I'm not an expert at doing any of this, but I try to do it at least adequately, and I enjoy making decisions. When is it time to make the genoa smaller on its furler, when is it time to reef that mainsail? What angle is best in a large chop when sailing on the wind? How long should each tack be?

I find that sailing is all about real-time feedback. It matters in the now how you sail. There is always a consequence for not getting things right, of not noticing a wind shift or a rise or decrease in wind speed. If your actions are not good enough, you get punished immediately by going into irons, or being gybed, or heeling over too far, or rounding up in a strong gust, or simply not getting the boat going very well at all, such as pointing too high and not generating enough boat speed to push through choppy seas.

Even in stable conditions when the autohelm basically does most of the work for sometimes hours at a time, there's always something to watch and listen for, and occasionally adjust. And there is always the GPS to fiddle with.

For me it is not a time for contemplating the meaning of existence, or mental repose, or nodding off – that's for when the anchor goes down. Perhaps I'm too nervous, especially when sailing alone. But I like to know what's happening, all the time. It's my active time. I can happily stand in the cockpit all the way to Great Barrier Island, or Tutukaka (which might take all day), and feel fully engaged, even if I seldom touch the wheel. And of course I've always got a line over the stern, just in case a nice kahawai or skipjack tuna attacks the lure.

The only repair I've been forced to make at sea, and in about 20 knots of wind, was when the ancient starboard genoa sheet winch starting slipping badly. It sounded as if all the cogs were shot. Not good. Because I had to tack into the wind on this particular route for many hours, I started putting the starboard sheet around the broken winch and taking it across to the port winch. Which was a good solution once I got my head around a different tacking routine. But then I saw that the starboard winch was braced to take a forward strain and not a sideways one, for the wooden cockpit coaming was flexing inwards somewhat.

I tied a blue plastic sheet along the safety rails to stop any bits from hurtling overboard, and dismantled the winch. Everything looked perfect, which is always a worry when you know that something is radically wrong. I had a screwdriver in my hand, tapping and prodding. Nothing amiss. Then for some reason or other I put it onto one of the large interior base screws, which looked firmly snugged, and was amazed to get a couple of turns, as was the case with the other two screws. That looseness had created just enough movement in the main spline to cause the cogs to slip under strain. Within minutes the winch was back together and all was well.

I find solo sailing particularly exciting because my senses are heightened just that much more. If I'm nervous I'm also mentally energised and, I hope, very careful and calculating. I'm more conscious of the 'what if' scenarios. I wear my PLB (personal locator beacon) on my belt, instead of leaving it in the grab bag, and also a razor-sharp knife in a pouch. I have an unbroken rule of never going forward out of the cockpit without being tethered to the webbing jackstays that run along the cabin top, no matter how gentle the winds and sea state. If I do get lucky and have to pull in a fish caught on the trailing lure, I always tether myself to the back stay, and there is always a sheathed knife attached to a rear stanchion if my catch is too big. I wish …

In my acts of sailing I'm neither timid nor reckless. I don't take risks with bad weather. I also like to think that I have a sensible confidence and a basic capability that readily lets me do solo runs to Great Barrier Island, the Bay of Islands and beyond to as far north, so far, as Houhora.

Insignificant rocks?

Channel Island is a tiny lump of rock in one of the windiest and roughest places in the Gulf, perpetually swept by strong tidal rips, just off the end of Coromandel Peninsula in the Colville Channel. It is probably best known to boaties because it is the first of the Nowcasting stations in the endlessly repeated sequence of VHF

Nowcasting reports – 'Channel Island, peak 36, average 30, from 145.' It is 77 metres high, circular, steep and with a mostly sheer rocky waterline it is very hard to land on. It has a light which flashes twice every 12 seconds. From a distance it can look like a shark fin, or a tooth, sticking up from the sea.

We have never sailed very close to it for it is not a good place for yachts to visit, but on the ferry from Tryphena to Auckland I once came within a few hundred metres. But it is a useful reference mark when sailing to Great Barrier Island, as it moves slowly across the face of the Colville Channel and eventually gets lost against the backdrop of the Coromandel Peninsula as the Barrier approaches.

As Cook's *Endeavour* sailed close by Channel Island, it was chased and attacked by stone-throwing warriors who had paddled out from the end of the Coromandel peninsula in a state of high consternation. Cook drove them away with musket fire. Unknown to Cook, the reason for Maori distress was that a mauri – a small and extremely sacred stone, a kind of talisman – had been deposited on the island by a high priest of the legendary *Arawa* canoe. Supposedly brought from Hawaiiki, the stone protected all Te Arawa members and their descendants from evil. Maori were angry that Cook was blundering into a most tapu place.[27]

The practice of placing mauri on tiny Gulf islands (and elsewhere) was common enough. Another sacred location was tiny Tikapa, now known as Gannet Rock, off the north-eastern tip of Waiheke Island. A mauri named Marutūahu was kept here. The Maori equivalent of Hauraki Gulf, Tikapa Moana, takes its name from this scrap of land. This particular mauri is now in the Auckland War Memorial Museum. Today Gannet Rock is probably best known as a good fishing spot, as well as a major gannet-breeding colony.

Most tiny scraps of dry land have significance. Throughout the Hauraki Gulf there are numerous islets and outcrops of rock that are major breeding grounds for wildlife, and host a wide range of flora. There's a delightful study by Mike Lee of seven islets off Waiheke. He recorded some 60 native plant species. Most have prolific bird life, especially during the breeding season. Lee lists some 14 native seabird species, and three native land birds.

One islet that intrigues me is tiny Koi island at the entrance to Rocky Bay. Numerous species of seabirds nest there, but notably it is the largest breeding colony in the inner Gulf of the red-billed gull. The main Gulf breeding colony for them is on the Mokohinau islands. We commonly assume that these 'sea gulls' are a non-endangered species since we see them everywhere, but their numbers overall, like most of our seabirds, are in significant decline. While these islets and others elsewhere have generally been less disturbed than larger islands by physical human presence, most nevertheless were commonly overrun by rats and mice and exotic weeds (including the odd marijuana plant), and thoughtless people who take dogs there create havoc for nesting birds.[28]

Apparently insignificant and inhospitable lumps of rock can have a variety of human perceptions and uses, as well as critical roles in nature. We only see what we know. And if we don't understand the cultural and natural importance of what we see, then we fail to appreciate the real value that is potentially all about us.

Dolphins, whales, orca, sharks

Everyone boating in the Hauraki Gulf has probably had the pleasure of dolphins playing round them – whether the common New Zealand dolphin or the larger bottle nose dolphin. The New Zealand dolphin is often in quite large groups. Dolphins always make people smile. They seem to be in good numbers throughout the Gulf, and often appear in harbours, even marinas, and close to mainland beaches as well as out to sea.

As a sea kayaker I have had a great many encounters with dolphins, but sitting so low on the water and being so small compared to the speedy dolphins, which always seem huge, it was always just slightly nerve wracking. Had they wanted to they could have demolished me in seconds. I enjoy encounters more from the yacht deck, and of course I can see more, including their bow riding – not something suited to a sea kayak.

My best dolphin encounter was sailing from Tiritiri Matangi to the bottom end of Waiheke – they played around our yacht for almost two hours. I almost got tired of watching them.

My greatest fear on the yacht (apart from falling off while sailing solo on autopilot) is hitting something, especially whales. There is a resident Gulf population of over 200 Bryde's whales (pronounced Broodahs), and sometimes they are joined by visitors. You don't often see the whales, but we've seen a few tails and a few spouts in the distance. I've also seen some cases of 'spy hopping' in the Colville Passage in which the whales stick their heads straight up out of the water for several seconds to spy for schools of fish and plankton that might be indicated even at a distance by birds working.

But they have this dangerous habit of sleeping or resting just under the surface where you can't see them. They are alleged to spend up to 90 per cent of their time very near the surface. Once, coming back from the Far North, I had close encounters with three of them. One was just north of the Bay of Islands. I happened to look down just beside the yacht and there was this massive white creature with long grooves in its skin – it was a Bryde's whale half rolled over looking up at me. They are rorqual whales and have multiple long groves in their under jaw and neck enabling their lower jaw to expand, a bit like a pelican's, to suck in a huge volume of water and fish to be filtered through baleen plates. They are not toothed whales.

A day or so later, coming across Bream Bay the yacht went between two of them, very close together, also showing their large area of white grooves, just a few metres either side of the boat, just under the surface.

I was very scared, and so thankful that I had not hit one of them.

They are of course a protected species. But this behaviour near the surface makes them very vulnerable to large ships travelling at speed. To stop the increasing number of fatal injuries to the whales by ships' propellers, all large vessels coming into Auckland since 2013 have been requested to reduce speeds and not to approach Auckland through the Craddock Channel, between Little Barrier and Great Barrier. The recommended entry route from the north is now the Jellicoe Channel, between Little Barrier and the mainland. The number of reported whale strikes has been reduced.

And that's another potential hazard for us. Previously the chances of getting near a ship in the outer Gulf were fairly slight, but now they are channelled into a smaller space we encounter them quite frequently crossing the Jellico Channel on the way from Kawau to Great Barrier. On at least two occasions when they have been heading straight for us I've been on the verge of calling them up on channel 16 on the VHF to ask if they can see me and what their intentions are. In both cases they did see me, adjusted course well in advance and passed a long way away. I assume our wooden yacht gives a poor radar return, so I have a cunning plan to hold up a cast-iron frying pan to give any large ship a good radar ping – although I have not yet quite felt the need to try.

Not too long ago there used to be humpback whales passing through the Hauraki Gulf, and elsewhere around New Zealand, on their way north from the Antarctic to their breeding ground in the tropical Pacific, but they are rare now, having been slaughtered by highly mechanised whaling practised by whaling nations. But there were still enough, it seemed, to justify opening a whaling station at Whangaparapara Harbour on Great Barrier Island as recently as 1956. It was a short-lived venture due to intensified whaling in the Antarctic and elsewhere, and it closed down in 1962.

There are probably still a few migrant whales visiting Great Barrier. After spending a day anchored under Mt Overlook on Kaikoura

Island we headed out into Port Abercrombie. Looking back, Merrilyn spied a large whale taking up our former position close to the shore.

I had two very close encounters with orca in the sea kayak. Once was in Queen Charlotte Sound when I was with a large group of sea kayakers. A large pod swam right around us, then underneath. I stayed firmly in the centre of our group. The other occasion was when I was alone, sea kayak fishing off the Browns Bay Reef. Two swam right past me. I had to look up to see the top of the large one's dorsal fin. It loomed like a submarine conning tower. The creatures were much longer than my kayak. I was not very relaxed. We have not had any orca encounters or sightings in the Gulf on our yacht.

However, we have seen many orca from the shore on Auckland's east coast beaches. Almost every winter they enter the Gulf and harbour and feast on stingrays, or 'orca biscuits'.

The Hauraki Gulf is a very sharky place. Indeed, New Zealand has 112 species of shark out of a world's total of 400. As a long-distance coastal sea kayaker I had plenty of encounters with sharks, fortunately none physically threatening, though all terrifying. They have swum under and around me. And a good friend had a paddling companion attacked by a great white on the crossing from Woolleys Bay to Whananaki in Northland, a route I have done scores of times. The shark came from below, knocked him out of the kayak, then kept away, enabling my friend to haul his mate back into his kayak. The teeth left an outline of the massive jaws on the bottom of the kayak, but because it was plastic the holes self-sealed. The pair fled to shore.[29] As soon as my friend got home he phoned me with the most graphic account. My latent 'Jaws' terrors instantly surfaced, and remain there still.

I have seen fewer shark fins from the yacht than from the kayak – I suppose the angles are different, and on the open coast in a kayak one is perhaps more observant and alert to such things. But we do sometimes see shark fins, or the shape of sharks just below the surface. One shape that is instantly recognisable is the hammerhead shark. We have seen several. It's nice to be in a safe yacht cockpit, presumably out of harm's way. More disturbing is the number of times after we have been swimming around the boat in an anchorage we have looked over the side and seen a big black shape casually cruising past. The most frightening was when it happened three times in three days on an extended stay in FitzRoy, Great Barrier Island, in 2015. The sharks were all very large bronze whalers. On the third occasion I managed to use my GoPro video camera on a pole to film the beast underwater. That ended our habit of the daily swim around the boat for some weeks.

The only obviously aggressive shark we have seen was when hauling in a large kahawai on a trailing lure just north of Tiritiri Matangi. The shark chased it all the way up to the stern of the boat, and when I lifted the kahawai out of the water the shark lunged up and sliced off the tail. That gave me a bit of a fright.

Rakino

Rakino literally translated means island of doom, thought to be a traditional reference to the tumult of the Rangitoto eruption. It's no longer a doomed island though it is a rather strange one.

The privately owned island is mostly open pasture and, except around Home Bay in the south, is largely surrounded by steep hillsides and cliffs. It was cleared of Norway rats in 2002, but there is no organised replanting scheme. For boaties it offers reasonable anchorages in popular Woody and West Bays on its western side and, in very settled weather, in Maori Garden Bay on the east. There is often good fishing around its rocky shores, especially where there is relatively deep water close along its north and north-eastern shores. There are some nice mussel caches too.

But on the island itself there's a slightly unreal scattering of some 70 modest dwellings spread along a central road, with a hardy resident population of fewer than 20. Wandering along the road past all the empty houses gives the place an unnerving *Mary Celeste* feeling. Everything seems normal. But there's no one there. One of the major problems for house owners is the lack of any effective ferry service, which is both a cause and an effect of the miniscule resident population. This is either good or bad depending on how you look at it. Rampant 'development' is not likely, but an almost complete lack of basic amenities – no mains water, sewerage or electricity – means that only the most practical and self-contained people live there permanently.

Rakino is thus mainly a land destination only for existing house owners who mostly use their dwellings as baches. For a few weeks in high summer the land population might swell to a hundred or so. Some of them use the most amazing collection of unregistered, unwarranted and altogether wonderfully decrepit motor transport to get to and from the wharf. But for most of the year the island has few people on it. One ultra-modern luxury hilltop residence – Hurakia Lodge, seemingly unoccupied – is at the south-western end. As I write, it is for sale. The sales pitch assumes prospective buyers will come and go via its helipad. As you do.

Rakino does have its moments – summertime community-organised dragon-boat racing, art exhibitions and music events. But mostly it's a deserted place.

Rakino was never intended to be a backwater. Governor George Grey bought the island in 1862 and starting to build a grand home for himself in Home Bay. But then Kawau came on the market and he bought that and moved there instead. In the 1870s Grey leased Rakino to Albert Sanford, who built the homestead now in Home Bay, farmed the island and fished. He used to row a boat 20 kilometres to the bottom of Auckland's Queen Street, where he sold his catch. The Sanford family was on the island for some 80 years, and ultimately created the Auckland-based Sanford seafood company, one of New Zealand's largest fishing and aquaculture ventures.

In the 1920s and 30s there was occasional newspaper discussion about the possibility of Rakino being developed as a public park, rather than Motuihe which was also the designated quarantine station. Nothing came of the idea.

Rakino looked set for a dramatic change in its fortunes in 1963 when it was bought by Dr Maxwell Rickard, who described himself as a 'clinical and educational psychologist', with a string of American degrees. He ran a nightclub in Auckland, toured the country as the hypnotist 'The Great Ricardo', and lectured, wrote books and made LPs on marriage and sex, self-hypnosis and 'miracles of the mind'.

As self-proclaimed President of the United Peoples' Organisation (World Wide) Incorporated, he planned to turn the island into a utopia caring for the less fortunate, and maybe even into a republic. Of course these naïve dreams never materialised. When Shirley Maddock interviewed him in his early time as Rakino's owner, during research for her classic book *Islands of the Gulf*, he was simply hoping to build a hotel. But he subdivided the island and sold it in 1965.

Rickard then seems to have gone to Australia, continuing to lecture and sell his wares there, and was doing so in the US in the 1980s. I recently saw some of his LPs for sale in New Zealand on Trade Me. The seller seemed slightly puzzled as to what they were. They went unsold.

Kawau – industrial landscape[30]

Copper Mine Bay at Kawau is a lovely anchorage, nestled against the overgrown kanuka hillsides, the shoreline fringed with huge pohutukawa. It is overlooked by the ruins of the old mine pump house with its gaunt brick chimney rising incongruously out of the natural landscape. There is little now to indicate the bustling miners' settlements and the greed, skulduggery and dirty industrial reality of the early mining enterprise on Kawau.

In 1852 'A Voyager' wrote a somewhat droll account of visiting Kawau. Passing nearby Motuketekete Island, the 'puff puff of the engine of the smelting furnace apprised us that the hand of the diligent maketh rich'. At Copper Mine Bay there 'was a busy scene of active industry; the high pressure engines working away with that spasmodic energy so characteristic of the railway locomotive, and so like a piece of plodding humanity wrapped up in its own importance and bluster'.

Around the corner and into Bon Accord Harbour our voyager came across smelting houses whose 'sulphurous exhalations were importing a barren and desolate aspect to all the vegetation within its influence'.[31]

Thus had the British industrial revolution reached a remote island in a remote new country.

With its relatively large land area and close proximity to the mainland Kawau was, like Waiheke, keenly sought by Maori. And the sheltered waters of Kawau Bay and the Mahurangi region teemed with fish, especially the small spotted sharks that were netted in their thousands and preserved by drying in the sun.

Among the early permanent settlers were Ngāi Tai. They were pushed out by Kawerau tribes, who in turn were challenged by the Marutūahu people, especially Ngāti Pāoa, during the 18th century, keen to exploit the shark fishery. By the late 18th and early 19th centuries Ngā Puhi raids from the north saw much of the island abandoned.

The North British Australian Loan and Investment Company purchased Kawau in 1840 from Ngāti Pāoa in a rather dubious sale. The Scottish-based company intended to farm the island, but when traces first of manganese and then of copper were discovered it formed the Kawau Company. This was run by John Taylor who then engaged (mining) Captain James Ninnis from Cornwall to manage the copper-mining enterprise. Ninnis brought a few Cornish families out with him, but contrary to popular belief there was no significant migration of workers from Cornwall. Most were typically transient colonial miners and labourers.

Soon this part of the Kawau coastline was dotted with the cottages and workshops of some 250-300 miners and their families. Ninnis had a house built for him (later George Grey's house) and a whole street full of lesser houses on the land behind. There were settlements elsewhere in bays in Bon Accord Harbour, as well as in Blackwoods Bay (now Dispute Cove) and Copper Mine Bay adjacent to the mine. The latter also had stables for the horses working the whims, machine shops, an engine house, a chapel and a school. A smelting works was built in Smelting House Bay in Bon Accord Harbour with its workers, some of whom were Welsh, housed some distance away in Swansea Bay to escape the fumes.

The enterprise never ran smoothly. First there were problems with shipping raw copper ore, which tended to heat up given its high sulphur content and become potentially combustible in a ship's hold. So the smelting works were constructed to create a more stable product.

Then there were the appalling actions of Frederick Whitaker and Theophilus Heale, who found out that the Kawau Company had rights only above high water so sunk a shaft – known as Whitaker's shaft – in the intertidal zone just metres away from the existing workings. Whitaker also constructed a workshop to service his ore extracts on dry land already reclaimed by the Kawau Company. He then built a rival smelter and settlement on Motuketekete Island, ferrying his workers across to Kawau every day.

But Whitaker's shaft ultimately doomed the entire enterprise. The only thing that stopped sea water sloshing into it was a wooden collar that rose above high tide. Whitaker also illegally dug inland, below sea level, into the existing mine workings, with the two companies inevitably breaking into each other's shafts. Can you imagine the drama? At that point all the mine shafts and tunnels were potentially connected to the sea and so were fatally compromised.

There were several years of bitter legal wrangling, leading to interventions by Governor George Grey. The Supreme Court eventually ruled against the grant to Whitaker and Heale but they appealed to

Earl Grey, Secretary for State for the Colonies in Britain, who advised reinstatement of their grant, which was done, to George Grey's chagrin.

But on the ground the situation was untenable. To protect the mine from flooding, both sides would necessarily have to trespass on each other's properties. The negotiated solution was that the Kawau Company bought out Whitaker and Heale's mining interest for 5000 pounds. As compensation the New Zealand government guaranteed the company that 'no portion of the fore-shore of the Island of Kawau shall henceforth be granted away by the Crown … ' and that the original grant to the company be extended to low-water level. Seabed and foreshore issues in modern New Zealand have long antecedents.[32]

Whitaker went on to become one of New Zealand's more prominent lawyers and businessmen, was a leading politician, had two periods as Premier, or Prime Minister, and was New Zealand's first Attorney General. Heale similarly had a career in politics and business, and was a Provincial Chief Government Surveyor and judge of the Native Land Court.

Keeping the mine dry had always been a critical problem since the ore was mostly well below sea level. A variety of steam pumps were employed, but eventually the mine flooded completely in 1852. A larger pump was commissioned and the (now-ruined) Cornish pump house was built in 1854 to drain the mine through Whitaker's shaft. Digging resumed but soon hard rock was reached. The copper lode was more limited than expected. There were also ongoing problems with labour given the better opportunities offered by gold mining in Coromandel and California.

It all got too hard and uneconomic. The mine was abandoned in 1855. The pump house whose remains we see today operated for only one year. In all some 3000 tons of copper ore had been extracted during the mine's life.

Shortly afterwards, Kawau's very own gunpowder plot took place when a party of Te Tawera Maori from Manaia arrived one night in three ships and stole over 2300kg of powder from the poorly secured mining company store. It took lengthy missionary and government intervention to have it returned.

The mining infrastructure is now long gone, except for the remains of the pump house. Whitaker's shaft, with a modern concrete collar and a steel-mesh safety grill, is still prominent right at the end of the pump house. The mining foreshore of reclaimed land has largely subsided back into the sea. In the kanuka on the ridge above the pump house it is said that you can still find a flattened circular area where horses walked round and round turning the whim that lowered and raised men, machines and ore in the shafts. With a copy of Captain Ninnis's 1848 sketch of the mine works and its surrounds in our hands (the map is readily available in free Department of Conservation pamphlets on Kawau) we have searched for it without success. But we did find a gaping vertical shaft in the bush, wisely fenced off by DOC.

Dispute Cove is mostly overgrown and is covered in massive pohutukawa trees toppled in some raging storm. In Copper Mine Bay there remains a clearing, covered in moss-like grass, and the foundation outlines of the old buildings can still easily be seen on the ground. Some can be identified from the Ninnis plan.

In Bon Accord Harbour only a few partial walls remain of the large smelting house, standing beside the Lidgard house near the Kawau Yacht Club. Behind these ruins is a large, ridged corrugated-iron roof seemingly resting on the ground. This is the site of a former building, almost the same size as the smelter, which housed machinery and other paraphernalia. The Department of Conservation has covered these remains with the roof to protect them. There is no entry. If DOC ever gets the funds, these industrial remnants may be displayed at some stage.

Kawau - Mansion House Bay[33]

Mansion House Bay is usually packed with moored craft eager to get as close as possible to George Grey's imposing mansion on the beach front, whereas Two House Bay, just several hundred metres away, is often shunned as an anchorage. And indeed it is not pretty. Mansion House Bay looks into the manicured lawns, exotic trees and Grey's elegant house. Two House Bay is partly surrounded by steep hills slipping into the sea, taking with them trails of dozens of fallen ugly pines. But we like it and often anchor there. And we can still see Mansion House.

Grey looms large in mid and later-19th century New Zealand. He was Governor of South Africa, South Australia, had two periods as Governor in New Zealand and ended up as Premier. It was he who launched the invasion of the Waikato with 10,000 imperial troops against the Maori King movement in the 1860s. Yet he also was a major student and benefactor of Maori. He learned the language, hob-nobbed with Maori leaders, studied their traditions and histories, and left a huge legacy of scholarship on matters Maori, particularly their myths and legends. His vast library, which also featured invaluable books and manuscripts covering literature, music, science and history, as well as his own huge personal correspondence, now forms the basis of the modern Grey Collection in the Auckland Public Library. Maori variously viewed and view him with a mix of contempt and utmost respect.

As we've seen, Grey's house on Kawau had been originally built in the 1840s for James Ninnis, manager of the copper mine. Grey purchased it in 1862, along with the whole island. The house was much more modest then, originally consisting of just a part of what is now the west wing. Grey made extensive additions, turning it into a grand mansion. Today the house, long since called Mansion House, and its manicured grounds look so incongruous in an island landscape of kanuka and overgrown pine trees. It would be a real shock to come around the corner and see it if you were not aware of its existence.

Grey was an active practitioner of acclimatisation, a 19th century movement which thought that it was noble to introduce plants and animals from other parts of the world to new locations. So Grey brought to Kawau possums, wallabies and kookaburras from Australia, as well as monkeys, zebra, deer, elk, turkey, wild pig, emu, antelope and peacocks. The monkeys used to annoy him with their early-morning chatter in the tree outside his bedroom so one day he got out his shotgun and despatched them. He also brought in the native weka.

The possums, wallabies, kookaburras and peacocks are still there. Indeed, possums are throughout New Zealand in plague proportions, though there were others as well as Grey who brought them into the country to create a fur industry. We often see wallabies when wandering through the bush tracks on the island. Peacocks strut about the house grounds. Weka are everywhere.

He introduced hundreds of plant species, most of which are no longer there, though in the Mansion House grounds there are still a considerable number of exotic palms and trees from all over the world. On the Redwood Track, going inland from Two House Bay, is a large American sequoia, hence the track's name. Alas he also started radiata-pine plantations, which have now run amok, creating a modern forestscape especially over the south of the island of giant, twisted trees which have poisoned the soil with their pine needles and are a serious hazard, toppling over during storms.

Grey lived the life of some sort of paternalistic baron, employing some 20 or more gardeners, farmers, labourers and servants whom he housed with their families in cottages scattered about the locality. These homes are now mostly gone. Grey had much of the peninsula on the southern side of Bon Accord Harbour cleared of remaining bush and turned into farmland.

He brought many international visitors to Kawau. English historian J.A. Froude in his *Oceana, or England and Her Colonies* (1886) probably accurately caught Grey's style:

> *There he lives amidst his intellectual treasures, in the midst of dependents who look on him more as a father than master; his house is always open to men of science, to the superior colonists, to strangers who have a better purpose than curiosity in seeking his acquaintance. A weekly post brings his letters and the periodic literatures of Europe.*[34]

While Grey strode the colonial political stage he and his wife Eliza had an unhappy personal life. Their only child died as a baby. During his South African governorship, on a return voyage to Cape Town from England on HMS *Forte*, he found that Eliza was flirting with the ship's captain, Rear Admiral Sir Henry Keppel. Grey assumed the worst, probably wrongly, and had her put ashore at Rio de Janeiro and sent back to London. He refused to speak to her or even of her until there was an unhappy reconciliation 36 years later.

Grey sold the house along with the island in 1888. The dwelling then had a long succession of owners. Early the next century a very large guest house was built adjacent to it on the beach front. From old photographs it looks almost as big as Mansion House, but it burned down after a few years. By the 1960s Mansion House was in considerable disrepair and was little more than a bar and doss house. It was taken over by the Hauraki Maritime Park in 1967, and from the 1970s renovation and restoration began. After 1991 it was transferred to the Department of Conservation and has received further restorative work to return it and its surrounds to something of their former glory. DOC administers the surrounding land that forms the peninsula south of Bon Accord Harbour, once Grey's farmland, as the Kawau Island Historic Reserve. The rest of the island remains in private ownership.

Kawau – wallaby woes[35]

Kawau is monotonously covered in kanuka (and the smaller manuka). This is the result of Grey's imported wallabies. Four species thrived, often in plague proportions – the dama or tammar, parma, swamp and brush-tailed rock wallaby. They are voracious eaters of most vegetation, except notably kanuka and manuka, kawakawa, some ferns and Arum lilies. Under the kanuka canopy not much else can survive. Without wallaby browsing a range of tree seedlings would eventually emerge through the kanuka and cover it to form a more 'normal' bush. But any emergent tree species currently have little chance of survival. Kawau thus has a perpetual near-monoculture of kanuka. Under this canopy there is little or no under-storey. The ground is often typically bare and exposed, which aggravates sediment run-off into streams and the sea. The tens of thousands of wallaby have also doomed all attempts at pastoral farming by nibbling away the grass. As well, the limited range of plant species means less available sustenance for native bird life.

Another issue with the island's vegetation is the wild pinus radiata that originated with Grey's plantations and which have spread over much of the southern regions of the island and beyond. They are the island's most invasive weeds. Now aged and often misshapen, they are a hazard in storms. When they do crash to the ground, and they do so very regularly, they open the canopy to the skies potentially making space for new plant species, but they have poisoned the soil with thick carpets of needles, and, anyway, wallaby will destroy most new plant life.

There have long been suggestions that the pine trees should be removed, but the expense and the collateral damage are major obstacles. In addition there are arguments that the pines are part of the historic landscape and should be left alone.[36]

Walking Kawau's tracks is not like walking through native New

Zealand bush. Rather it is like travelling through strange forest scenes from *Lord of the Rings*.

But we love the walks out from Mansion House Bay. Our routine is to walk the Old Coach Road starting behind Grey's house to the copper mine remains. From the high point on the track on the way there are magnificent views over Beehive Island and beyond. Then the descent via a cliff side track into Dispute Cove and the rocky coastal section to the mine pump house. Back up the steep road and down the Redwood Track, which is a favourite trail. In spite of the pine canopy there are magnificent ferns and a gurgling stream. But it is annoying to come across signs which say 'Historic Site' without telling you what it is, or was. The few old bricks lying about give no indication that they are the remains of Grey's dairy cottages and cool stores. There are old photographs of these cottages set amidst open pasture. Why can't a few copies be put onto signs on the spot, now darkly covered with vegetation?

By the 1970s it was slowly accepted that Kawau was approaching ecological crisis. Apart from the wallabies, myriad possums were destroying many of the few remaining pohutukawa trees (as they were throughout the whole of Northland). But official action was slow.

Many Kawau property owners started to create their own initiatives. From the 1980s there was large-scale public trapping of possums, which has dramatically lowered their tree-stripping habits, and protected many of the last remaining stands of mature native trees.

One of the main advocates for controlling wallaby and possums is the Pohutukawa Trust New Zealand which was incorporated in 1992. It is principally funded and supported by the majority of the small resident population on Kawau. It has pushed hard for an effective eradication programme for wallaby and other pests and has government and local body agencies now supporting it, at least morally.

But the politics of wallaby eradication have been difficult. A minority of residents and others have been fierce opponents and the planned dates for eradication, originally set at 2005, have constantly been put back. New-generation poisons have proven to be safe and effective, but they have yet to be used systematically on an island-wide basis. There has been much localised use of approved poison by residents as well as shooting, both of which have reduced wallaby numbers. It is believed that the brush tail wallaby is now extinct. Some of the tammar population have been repatriated to Australia where the native originals are in decline.

But the chances of ever having a predator-free island seem daunting. In addition to possums and wallabies there are ship rats, feral cats and recently arrived stoats, as well as the introduced native weka which are aggressive predators on birds' eggs, young birds and lizards and have been known to kill stoats and rats.

And unlike other islands in the Gulf which are government controlled and can be closed off to the public to eradicate predators, Kawau is a large landmass and is 90 per cent privately owned. The Department of Conservation's own territorial control on Kawau is mainly limited to the historic reserve on the southern peninsula of Bon Accord Harbour, which is a tiny fraction of the island. Private owners have neither the resources, nor are at times able to reach sufficient agreement, to implement a total island-wide restoration programme.

Even if the Department of Conservation was enabled to go ahead with a planned mass eradication programme, opposition from some quarters would doubtless make life difficult in this litigious age.

So a wallaby population, while reduced, remains.

Kawau - sailing about

The joy of recreational sailing in Kawau Bay, that large area of sheltered sea between Kawau Island and the mainland, dotted with little islands, was appreciated even before Grey's time. It was and still is a major mecca for boaties. In less environmentally aware days it was claimed that so many beer bottles covered the bottom of Mansion House Bay that it was becoming difficult to set an anchor. Some of the glass has been subsequently cleaned out in scuba-diving operations.

There's also the additional opportunity to sail right round Kawau, and that never fails to please too. Our direction is somewhat dependent on where the wind is coming from, although I prefer anticlockwise, for no good reason. Starting from, say, Bon Accord Harbour, I like to track past the copper-mine remains and South Cove and through Rosario Channel. The warship HMS *Rosario* is best known for its investigations in the late 1860s and early 1870s into the labour trade in which Melanesian islanders were recruited as sugar plantation workers in Queensland and there were accusations that they were in fact being 'blackbirded', or kidnapped.

Probably more significant for New Zealand is the fact that a team from *Rosario* was the first 'international' side to play rugby in New Zealand, in 1870.

The run across Kawau's south coast offers a stop at the intriguingly named Bostaquet Bay. I always think of Tessa Duder's classic yachting story *Night Race to Kawau*. Bostaquet is a French Huguenot name and a particular person in Normandy has been tracked as a distant relative of Grey's mother. In his youth Grey had visited ancestral family locations in Normandy.[37]

Behind the bay is a particular grove of trees, allegedly a 'cannibal feasting hall' of early Maori. Grey took Froude to see it and he suitably shivered with horror at the spot. It's one of those old imperial cannibal tales that were commonly told in colonial days, and this one still has some popular currency, appearing in Tessa Duder's story and featuring in the commentary of passing commercial tourist vessels.

Years ago it was possible to wander the tracks from Bostaquet Bay to Bon Accord Harbour. Now the tracks are barred with locked gates and festooned with signs warning against trespassing on private land, claiming dangers from shooting of wallabies and poison baits.

The workers who built the light on Flat Rock, a reef three miles off Kawau's east coast, camped at this beach for a whole year, such was the infrequency of fine weather, to enable them to build a small concrete pillar on a rock barely above sea level. Even today light inspections of Flat Rock cannot always be undertaken because boat access is required and only calm-water landings can be attempted.

Tides around Challenger Island at Kawau's south-east tip can be swift and if there is little wind yachts need to be a bit wary. The dare-devil Erling Tambs who sailed with his wife from Norway to New Zealand in the early 1930s, with virtually no navigational charts or instruments, lost his engineless vessel *Teddy* when currents dragged it into Challenger.

The outside coast of Kawau is weather beaten, steep and rugged and there are many reefs. The only reasonable daytime anchorage, in settled weather, is Burgess Bay. A good place for a lunch break and a swim. Beyond Burgess Bay it's best to keep offshore a bit. I used to rock garden along this coast in my sea-kayaking days but sailing in a yacht is a different matter. However, no matter what I do I always seem to end up over or very close to Nelson Rock. Marked at a depth of 2.9 metres on the charts, it's no problem in calm seas for our 1.5 metre draught *Mercury*. But it annoys me that somehow I always gravitate towards it.

As the island tends north-west there's another calm-day anchorage just before Fairchild Reef. But there are few sunken rocks to look out for. The bay features a single cottage with giant sliding shutters that cover it entirely – either the storms can be extreme or vandals are sometimes about.

Entering North Channel can be interesting. There are strong tidal rips and sometimes swells. Whatever the wind direction elsewhere, it tends to funnel along the channel's east/west axis and is thus either on the nose or directly behind. I've had some long tacking duels sailing westwards into an outgoing tide and a westerly wind. I got a fright one day when I muffed a tack to port after going past Maori Rock, and the strong outgoing tide started taking me back towards it.

The worst entrance we had was on an outgoing tide with a strong tail wind and huge swells generated by some disturbance out at sea. It was best not to look behind.

The idea is to pass between Maori Rock to the north and Fairchild Reef to the south (you are in very serious trouble if you don't), then turn to port into the calm waters of Kawau Bay, but only when well past the lighthouse on Kawati Point to avoid further sunken reefs. The island now reverts to a gentle holiday-house coastline. Once past tiny Pembles Island, a port turn takes you into the safety of my beloved North Cove.

Kawau - North Cove

North Cove is small, hopelessly crowded with mooring buoys, very tidal and muddy, there is nowhere to land, and the hills are covered with dull scrub and kanuka. It has no attraction at all as a land destination. But it's very sheltered in all winds, and its intimate size seems to envelope me. I've seen out several storms there. I've always felt not only safe, but snug.

North Cove is in fact packed with interest. It is the adopted home of Lin and Larry Pardey, among the world's best known sailing couples. Their Lyle Hess-designed *Taleisin*, probably one of the most instantly recognisable cruising yachts, lay moored just off their wharf for decades until it was sold in mid-2015. I've taken dozens of photographs of it. Having read their books, plus the recent biography by Herb McCormick, and seen their videos, I have a sense of familiarity about their lives and adventures and their Kawau world. Lin's book *Bull Canyon* and Larry's *Details of Classic Boat Construction* provide the most amazing and moving details of *Talesin's* construction in an inland Californian canyon.

North Cove, thanks to the Pardeys, has become either a home or a well-used visiting and maintenance spot for a number of classic New Zealand boats. It is always pleasing to row around them in our tender.

On the opposite shore is Camp Bentzen, which provides outdoor education for school children, and endless entertainment for us. There are often parties of youngsters fishing and jumping off the wharf, and kayaking and small-boat sailing all about the bay. They are filled with chatter and laughter and shouting and energy, except when they disappear for meals and suddenly it all goes very quiet.

There are always water taxis fussing about, collecting or depositing residents and visitors on the little jetties.

There are two very shallow tidal estuaries at the head of the cove, which can be explored only by dinghy.

There are wonderful old cottages scattered around the cove, full of character, often a bit scruffy, but redolent of decades of family summer holidays. Alas the mega-wealthy have begun to move in around the deeper shores of the cove, building their predictable mega-dwellings, with large wharves and floating pontoons. A stay in the cove these days can sometimes be accompanied by the screech of circular saws and the banging of nail guns.

Browns Island/Motukorea

It's the best-known Auckland island landmark after Rangitoto, and probably the most loved. Plans to turn it into a sewerage plant in the 1940s were thrown out by public opposition, led by a feisty Dove-Meyer Robinson, later mayor of Auckland. Any suggestion even today that it might be planted in native trees receives the immediate disapproval of Aucklanders who like it just the way it is, sitting there all content at the Waitemata Harbour entrance. It looks a happy island, a smooth, softly shaped volcanic cone, covered in the greenest grass in winter and burned golden in summer. It has long looked like this. In 1827 Dumont d'Urville described it as 'almost completely covered with a thick carpet of very green grass'.[38]

Recent efforts by Ports of Auckland to extend container wharves further into the Waitemata Harbour have seen a howl of outrage from Auckland citizens, not just because of the environmental consequences of making the harbour more like a narrow drain but because such wharves and the massive container ships berthed there would block off people's beloved downtown views to Browns Island.

Yet few people actually go to the island. There are no ferries, and even private boats are restricted by its very shallow and rocky coastline. There is but one small calm-weather anchorage in Crater Bay.

Its age still has to be determined, but current thinking suggests that it was long ago, and certainly at a time when most of the Hauraki Gulf was well above sea level. Thus, unlike its much more recent Rangitoto neighbour, it did not emerge from the sea. Instead the rising ocean eventually turned it into an island. The two islands make a nice geological contrast – one looking old and worn smooth, the other new with sharp lava.

Motukorea, island of oystercatchers, was occupied by Ngāti Tamaterā who built defensive works around the summit cone and extensively gardened the island. Their ancient garden stone shelter walls are readily visible, though the ones built in long straight lines belong to later colonial farming. It was a base for extensive fishing activity, including large stone fish traps built in the shallow tidal reefs. There was also stone working for tools and utensils using local materials. Though Ngāti Tamaterā were generally acknowledged owners in 1840, other groups claim some interest in the island – the Hauraki tribes, Ngāi Tai and Ngāti Pāoa.

The island was strategically located. It guarded the entrance to the Tamaki River and the all-important portage to the Manukau Harbour and thus access to the west coast. It also commanded the seaways between the Waitemata Habour and all the inner Gulf islands, and beyond.

When it was rumoured that Hobson was moving the capital to Auckland, in 1840, two merchants then operating in the Coromandel area, William Brown and John Logan Campbell, bought the island from Ngāti Tamaterā as a speculative venture. They landed, had a Maori whare built for them, and were soon raising pigs and using the island as a trading base. Later in life Campbell wrote the now classic *Poenamo,* a kind of boy's-own adventure tale, reminiscing about his days of living simply and free on Motukorea and his early mercantile doings in the fledging town of Auckland.

One marvellous story concerns the arrival on the island one day, shortly after Brown and Campbell purchased it, of the country's 'Deputy Governor', Willoughby Shortland. According to Campbell, a Ngāti Whātua chief had 'gifted' the island to Governor Hobson as a way of enticing him to shift the capital to Auckland. He sent his deputy to raise the flag to claim it for the Crown and also to 'summarily bundle' two supposedly disreputable 'Pakeha-Maori' off the island by 'neck and crop'.[39] Instead he found two civilised Scotsmen plus the Ngāti Tamaterā chief who had sold them the island. The official realised that he had been misinformed and left after a fine feast and jolly time with Brown and Campbell.

Though the hole for the flagpole had already been dug at the summit, it was never raised, and the flag spar instead was abandoned on the beach where 'it lay until its sap rotted away, and then it yielded snatches of firewood to encamping Maories'.[40]

The visit confirmed to Brown and Campbell that Auckland was indeed to be the new capital:

> *Never more was the little island a place lying in mid-channel of waters which showed no signs of life, for now the raupo sail of the Maori canoe was rarely wanting, soon to be replaced by the calico sail, which, with white wings, dotted the surrounding waters and marked still more brightly that the expanse of the inlet leading from Te Hauraki to Waitemata had now become a great thoroughfare to the new home of the Pakeha.*[41]

Auckland was from the very first the City of Sails.

After some months Campbell moved to the mainland and Brown followed soon after, leaving his name on the island, though he kept ownership until 1873. Both became prominent Auckland merchants, with Campbell later in life creating a legacy as the Father of Auckland.

The rapid growth of Auckland saw Maori in the region reshape priorities to take advantage of commercial opportunities. For most of the next two decades Maori on the inner Gulf islands, the Coromandel and the Thames/Waikato region supplied Auckland's increasing population with fish and meat, fruit and vegetables of all kinds, maize, wheat, flour and firewood. Maori were in fact the biggest providers of food for the citizenry of New Zealand's largest town.

The Waitemata Harbour saw a remarkable canoe trade, peaking in the early 1850s with almost 2000 annual canoe arrivals. There was a similar trade via the Manukau Harbour by Waikato Maori. Enterprising tribes were soon buying schooners to provide even more goods. In 1858 there were over 80 vessels registered or licensed to Maori in the Auckland province.

As far as the Gulf islands were concerned, many supplied timber, often kauri, from Great Barrier Island, and the few remaining stands on Kawau and Waiheke. These islands as well as most inner Gulf islands provided fish, firewood, pigs and vegetables.

A good proportion of the trade was also stimulated by the Victorian gold rush in Australia, enabling Maori to be significant exporters across the Tasman. Maori were also considerable buyers of Western goodies with their new wealth, providing the Colonial Exchequer with about one third of its excise take in 1855.

But the end of the Australian gold rush saw a sudden and serious export market decline in New Zealand, and Maori never recovered.

It was not just this collapse that was a blow. There were also underlying structural problems for Maori tribes engaged in commerce. Many had borrowed heavily, especially for schooners and flour mills. And Maori were not yet good capitalists in that the wealth they generated was not always used to pay off debts or reinvested. Maori often dispersed their money with generous feasting and hosting.

But above all, Maori on the Gulf islands and in the Auckland region generally were largely landless by the 1860s, having sold their lands, sometimes to repay their debts and usually in deals that were sometimes dodgy and generally to their eventual disadvantage. In the Thames-Coromandel area Maori entered into gold agreements with the Crown that invariably led to land selling. Thus were they excluded from the new source of wealth. The future role of Maori in the colonial economy, if any, was essentially as landless labourers.[42]

Campbell bought out Brown's share of the island in 1873 and sold it in 1879. In 1906 it was purchased by the owners of the Devonport

Steam Ferry Company, the Alisons, who sold it in 1946 to the Auckland Drainage Board for its ill-planned sewerage plant. During the Alison tenure several of their old paddle-wheel steam ferries were left derelict on the island's shore. Old photographs show them like so many dead mechanical dinosaurs. It was also a time when the Alisons organised large public picnics with their ferries.

After the sewerage fiasco the island was bought by Ernest Davis (of Tiritiri Matangi lighthouse fame). He gifted it to 'the mayor, councillors and people of Auckland' in 1955. It is technically 'managed' by the Department of Conservation. In 2013 the Crown attempted to gift it to Maori as part of a Treaty settlement – until it was pointed out that the Crown did not own it.[43]

Dispossession

The beginnings of European settlement and colonial rule could not have come at a worse time for Maori, struggling as they were with the consequences of the musket wars. In the Hauraki Gulf and Auckland region communities (as elsewhere) were often fairly easy game for land buyers. While many, perhaps most, early land purchases were eventually legitimised in colonial law, the European buyers were only too well aware that they were getting the better deal, even though the sellers at the time might have expressed satisfaction, and indeed were often satisfied with what they were paid. Only later would the collective loss of land make most Maori realise that they had become virtually landless in their own country.

Moreover, negotiations with Maori were often with willing sellers rather than those who were not consulted and either did not know, or who might have been opposed. There was always the inherent problem or buying land where ownership was either shared or contested.

This has left a long legacy of bitterness.

The following simplified chart, based heavily on Paul Monin's research, gives a general idea of the alienation of the main islands.

	Pre or in 1840s	By 1865	By 1900
Browns	*		
Rangitoto	*		
Motuihe	*		
Motutapu	*		
Rakino	*		
Waiheke	*	*	*
Pakatoa/Rotoroa & Ponui	*	*	
Tiritiri Matangi	*		
Kawau	*		
Great Barrier	*	*	*
Little Barrier			*
Hen and Chickens			*
Mokohinau			*

All islands, apart from Waiheke and Great Barrier, were single sales. Most of the islands (some 88 per cent of the total land area) were sold before 1865.[44] This contrasts with much of the rest of Maori land in New Zealand, which was alienated mainly after the Land Court was established in that year.

The only significant land on Gulf islands in Maori ownership in the early 20th century was some 1200 hectares at Katherine Bay, Great Barrier.

Restitution?

The islands of the Hauraki Gulf, and the Auckland isthmus, were amongst the earliest areas of land to be bought from Maori, in the period immediately before and during the earliest days of colonial rule. But they have been among the final areas to be considered by the Treaty of Waitangi Tribunal (which was established in 1975). In 2015, as I write, there is much underway, but although in some instances Tribunal reports have been completed and some settlements are imminent, many other reports and settlements have yet to be finalised.

One new element, since 2009, has been the strategy of grouping claimants into collectives. This was necessary because, especially in the Hauraki Gulf and Auckland region generally, so much of the land was traditionally a patchwork of intertribal and hapu sharing as well as conflicting interest; dealing with any single group to the exclusion of others would be yet another injustice.

With regard to the extensive expert research findings, and the Tribunal reports completed, the general conclusion is that the Crown in this region as elsewhere in New Zealand breached its Treaty obligations. This happened especially by cavalier approval of many initial private sales, and by implementing its own direct, monopoly purchasing of Maori land in the time of Crown pre-emption (to 1865) without adequately investigating who really were the customary owners. Then there was a failure to properly protect Maori interests with the operations of the Native Land Court and other government actions after 1865.

Settlements (as at the end of 2015):

- The Waiheke settlement in 1989 involved the transfer of the 800 hectare Waiheke Station at the eastern end of Waiheke to Ngāti Pāoa.
- The Crown settlement with Ngāti Whātua Orakei was finalised in 2012 which included cultural, land and financial redress of $18 million.

- In 2014 the Tāmaki Makaurau Collective Redress Bill was passed into law. The Collective, comprising 13 Tamaki isthmus tribes and hapu, is to be vested with ownership of 14 volcanic cones and some small areas of land on the isthmus. As well they will be gifted Tiritiri Matangi, Rangitoto, Motutapu and Motuihe, and then within a month these islands will be re-gifted to the Crown. Maori will have an ongoing co-management role. This particular act does not settle historical claims. Each group within the collective will negotiate these individually with the Crown (as Ngāti Whātua above and Ngāi Tai below).
- In late 2015 Ngāi Tai received $12.7 million in financial and commercial redress, along with the vesting of certain Crown-owned scenic, historic and recreational sites in the Auckland region. Specifically on the Gulf Islands these are located on Motutapu, Motuihe, and Waiheke (Te Makutu Bay). There were also various region-wide deeds of recognition, including Stony Batter on Waiheke.

Current negotiations:

- Ngāti Manuhiri (related to Ngāti Wai) offered $9 million and some sites on Little Barrier nature reserve within a broader collective agreement.
- Settlement with Te Kawerau a Maki will be under Tamaki Makaurau Collective redress.
- Ngāti Rehua-Ngāti Wai has an agreement in principle, offering $4.6 million. The Mokohinau Islands will be gifted and regifted back to the Crown. There will be a transfer of ownership of Rakitu Island, the summit of Mt Hobson, Awana Recreation Reserve, Rangiwhakaia and other locations. There will be a deed of recognition in regard to Mokohinau Islands, Little Barrier and some parts of Great Barrier. Access to and management of Mokohinau muttonbirds will be negotiated.

- Report of the Hauraki Collective (a range of tribes mainly from the hinterlands around the Firth of Thames, and including Waiheke) was completed in 2006. Settlement is expected soon.
- The Marutūahu record of collective agreement (Ngāti Maru, Ngāti Pāoa, Ngāti Tamaterā, Ngāti Whanaunga, Te Patukirikiri) 2013 offers $30 million, plus potential cultural redress of Motuora Island, the historic reserve at Kawau and other reserve land at Mahurangi.
- Hearings before the Tribunal on the Mahurangi Purchase started in early 2014.

The amount of land on islands that can be returned will always be small because no private land can be used for settlement purposes. It must be limited to Crown land, which is now mostly reserve land. Then there is symbolic and legal recognition of prior customary rights to Gulf islands and locations, plus co-management of a range of issues. As well, significant amounts of money and other resources are intended to provide a substantial contribution towards a new economic base for claimants in recompense for cultural and historical land loss.

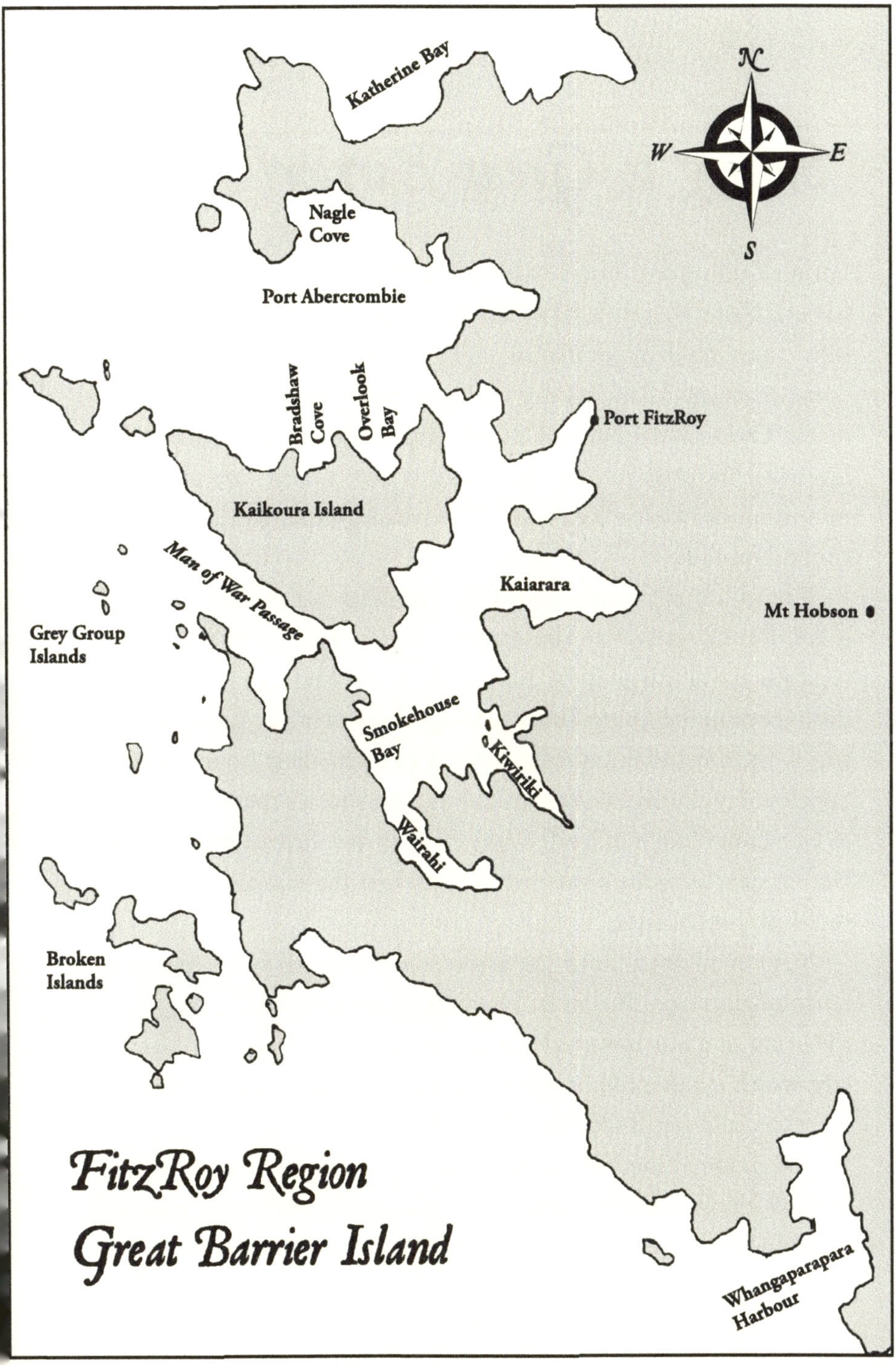

Katherine Bay
N
W
E
S
Nagle Cove
Port Abercrombie
Bradshaw Cove
Overlook Bay
Port FitzRoy
Kaikoura Island
Man of War Passage
Kaiarara
Mt Hobson
Grey Group Islands
Smokehouse Bay
Kiwiriki
Wairahi
Broken Islands
FitzRoy Region
Great Barrier Island
Whangaparapara Harbour

Sailing to Great Barrier/Aotea

For me, sailing to Great Barrier is the ultimate Hauraki Gulf destination. Great Barrier is how New Zealand used to be, all bush and hills, a tiny resident population and very little modern development. Some years ago I paddled my sea kayak from Fletcher Bay at the tip of the Coromandel Peninsula and then circled the island. I fell in love with the pristine coastline which is now a fairly rare phenomenon in much of New Zealand. We have also explored the island by car and on foot.

From Gulf Harbour to Great Barrier Island is about 40 nautical miles. It's not really very far when you consider that even slow yachts typically travel 100 nautical miles in 24 hours. And it's a much shorter distance than the run to Tutukaka – 67 nautical miles. Yet the Barrier trip is the most exciting because it takes us furthest from land. For hopeless day dreamers of ocean sailing, like me, it's the nearest thing to being out of sight of land. And on a hazy day there sometimes is no land in sight for quite some time. I always get the compass out just for fun. I play real sailing.

It is not always a quick sail across, indeed mostly we've found it a fairly long passage. The most favourable wind direction for sailing, on the beam, is a north-westerly, which is not common, or a south-easterly, which is more common but often brings with it a pretty bouncy sea, especially across Colville Channel.

The good old south-westerly is not always that useful on this route because it's right on the stern. And a stiff south-wester is not good for returning from the Barrier. Several times I've done no better than to head towards the bottom end of Waiheke, before angling across.

Sometimes we overnight on Kawau, and do the run to Great

Barrier passing Little Barrier the next day. A south-westerly works better on this angle.

The worst wind is none at all. The motor rumbles away for hours, and hours. I hate using the motor to get anywhere. It uses only a litre and a half an hour at five and a half knots, so it's not that. It's just that a yacht harnesses the wind, it is liberated and liberating when the sails fill and drive the vessel across the sea, it is primeval, utterly basic, yet also poetic.

Sailing to Great Barrier Island can be hypnotic, as slowly, ever so slowly, the mountain range rises to its full height above sea level, and features of the landscape change from a distant opaque to closer, dramatic detail. And the angles change relative to each other – Moehau eventually falls behind, Channel Island merges into Moehau, and Little Barrier slowly slides portside.

Traditional Pacific island navigators had a concept of ocean travel in which they regarded their canoes as stationary while it was the islands that moved. The trick was to operate and orient the canoe in such a way that the destination island came towards them. It's a good perceptual game to play sailing to Great Barrier.

Arrival at Great Barrier is exciting not just because it's the end of the longish trip, but because the entrance to Port FitzRoy is so fascinating and scenically dramatic. There's a bit of needle-threading through the wonderful islets of the Grey Group, and a sharp starboard turn into the channel running alongside Kaikoura Island, avoiding the dangerously placed Paget Rock. Then there's the run up to the Man of War Passage which is often hard to spot from any distance and when identified always seems so impossibly narrow. Once through, Port FitzRoy suddenly opens as if you have exited a tunnel into a new landscape of endless calm waters surrounded by wonderful native bush-clad hills, all overlooked by the dramatic peaks of Mt Hobson and Mt Heale.

Sailing back is equally fascinating. For a while there is no land visible ahead, then the tip of Rangitoto appears, and finally the vivid white lighthouse on Tiritiri Matangi pops up. I can't help thinking, fancifully I know, of Coleridge's ancient mariner finally in sight of his home:

Is this indeed
The light-house top I see?
Is this the hill? …
Is this mine own countree?

Great Barrier - Port FitzRoy

Port FitzRoy has a capital R, because Robert FitzRoy, after whom it was named, claimed royal status as the fourth (and illegitimate) great grandchild of Charles II. FitzRoy means 'son of a king', and was commonly applied to any of their illegitimate offspring. I have already mentioned Robert FitzRoy's role as New Zealand's second governor, the captain of the *Beagle* (with Darwin) and his founding of the British meteorological office.

I'm sure that he would not really like Port FitzRoy. In the early 19th century mind such a wilderness of bush and fold upon fold of jagged hills was seldom seen as a landscape fit for civilised pastoralism. There were the marvellous kauri to be felled, and some copper to be mined, but there was little else deemed worthy. But for us today the wild landforms and pristine scenery are precisely its attraction.

Port FitzRoy is a boaties' paradise with its almost completely landlocked expanse of sea, just like a lake. The only swells come from the speeding monster power boats. While most boats anchor, herd like, in a few key locations, like Forestry, Kaiarara, Wairahi, Kiwiriki and Smokehouse Bays, you can lower your pick almost anywhere else. We often anchor between the shore and one of several mussel farms. Since most other boats don't do this we get space to ourselves. The water by these farms is always quite deep, and proximity to the mussels makes fishing for the evening snapper more successful. Also the rows of the mussel farm buoys help dampen any boat wash heading our way.

The first night we tried this we were awoken at early dawn by loud knocking on the bottom of the boat. For a confused nanosecond I had stupid visions of some scuba diver playing a joke and knocking on our underwater door, then the slightly more rational thought that we had somehow drifted onto a cable anchoring the mussel farm. But when we got up and looked overboard there were three enormous kingfish bumping their heads against the hull. It has happened very many times since and always brings both joy at seeing these beasts and intense, instinctive frustration at not having any way to catch one.

Port FitzRoy anchorages are also notable for birdsong, even of a limited kind – the screeching of kaka during the day, and the haunting cry of morepork at night. There's always a sense of a bounteous nature, not often found elsewhere. The rocky shoreline abounds with oysters and mussels. There are boil-ups of bait fish and kahawai in season. Gannets perpetually patrol the skies. In the evening, again in season, the sea can literally come alive with millions of mackerel.

It is easy to spend a day at anchor doing nothing in particular, just watching nature and the passing parade of boats, having an occasional foray ashore to get a feed of oysters and mussels at low tide, swimming off the boat, lazily fishing and snoozing.

The feeling of utter anchoring security is strong, but it can be misleading. In seriously strong winds the surrounding mountains accelerate drafts to potentially damaging strengths. Our only anchor drag happened in Wairahi inlet in a seemingly completely sheltered spot. The wind came in huge gusts that you could hear roaring and rumbling before they hit. Mast and rigging vibrated, then the whole boat shook, and the wind took on an unnatural screaming noise. The yacht yawed in a demented way. It went on for almost four days.

Great Barrier Island, like the Coromandel Peninsula, which both have easterly aspects and high hills, can have extremes of bad weather with damaging winds and great downpours that can generate walls of water surging down steep gullies.

Sometimes we anchor by the wharf at Port FitzRoy, mostly to dump our rubbish, and also to watch the goings-on of people lured to the wharf for fuel and water and the shop for beer and newspapers. I admit to a sense of smugness when I see giant powerboats having to fill up with 1000 litres or more of diesel.

We usually chat to the delightful Kay Stowell, the island's information officer, who seems to spend her entire life in an 'office' not much bigger than an anchor locker. Noisy kaka and tui are also attracted in numbers to the human activity.

Among other interesting locals we have met are Sven and Trish Stellin, who run Barrier Gold at Wairahi, making oils, balms and soap from ti-tree (kanuka and manuka) oil. Sven is a tireless enthusiast when explaining his handpicking and processing of the tiny leaves. Huge volumes of leaves are required to produce even small quantities of the precious oil.

We sometimes go outside Port FitzRoy waters to vary the scene. Going out the northern entrance into Port Abercrombie we anchor in Nagle Cove, or Overlook Bay, or Bradshaw Cove. The high craggy shorelines are spectacular.

We make forays a bit further afield, north to Miners Cove and around the corner to the site of the wreck of the SS *Wairarapa* that slammed into sheer cliffs in 1894 with the loss of some 130 lives. About 100 managed to survive. It was a long and grisly job looking for bodies, some of which drifted around to the eastern side of the island. About 80 were eventually found. Some 60 were unknown or unrecognisable due to shark bites and were buried on the island in mass graves at Onepoto in Katherine Bay and at Tapuwai at Whangapoua. Others were buried at Rakitu (Arid) Island and Harataonga. The grave sites are now tended by the Department of Conservation. Those bodies that could be identified were sent to Auckland for burial.

Going southwards from Port FitzRoy we like Oneura Bay. Using a bottom-bait rig the last time there, I hooked a giant kingfish which stripped the line off my inadequate reel and eventually did a massive aerial leap before breaking off. I had been led to believe that kingfish only ever take live bait, and would never leap out of the water. I have since upgraded my gear and await a repeat kingfish experience.

Then we go further south, sailing through the Grey Group Islands and the aptly named Broken Islands with their organic volcanic sculpturing, and beyond to Whangaparapara Harbour.

And always in the region is the overpowering presence of the hills and their sharp volcanic peaks.

Great Barrier – the grid at Smokehouse Bay

In my youth there were drying grids or piles at many beaches in Auckland. Yachts and launches would tie up at high tide, settle at low water to enable boat owners to work (for free) on their hulls, and float off on the flood tide. I loved spending long holiday days at Duders Beach at Devonport picnicking with my mum, watching boaties work on the tidal grids at the yacht club.

Today there are virtually no grids left. The 'authorities' now see only dangers for boat owners, though I'm sure no boat ever fell over. Moreover, they are paranoid about avoiding even the smallest splash of antifoul. It is also darkly hinted that marina operators opposed grids because they want you to use their hellishly expensive lift-out cranes.

Our Townson 30 has a Kiwi feathering prop that requires lubricating every six months, plus a replacement prop anode at the same time.

Mostly I get an eye-wateringly expensive half-hour lift-out and hold at the marina. It's a frantic rush to get the job done within 30 minutes, and if you run over time you are charged the hourly rate.

But there is still a grid – on a tiny beach at Smokehouse Bay at Great Barrier Island. If the prop lube job is due when I am there, and if the tide is right, and if nobody else is on it, then I go for it.

The facility is provided by the Webster family, which also maintains a self-operated wood-fired hot-water bath house, fish-smoking and clothes-washing facilities complete with outside tubs, ancient mangles and rotary clothes lines. All they ask is a donation in the box.

The place is impossibly crowded at peak holiday times, but otherwise you can pretty much have it to yourself.

My last time on the grid was in May, late in the season, yet it was almost like summer and not a breath of wind. Nobody was about. And what a joy it was. The location in Port FitzRoy with the surrounding forested volcanic peaks, the bush down to the shoreline – which in turn is covered in mussels and oysters – and the birdsong is inspiring. If you face away from the tubs and mangles it's like looking at New Zealand before humans arrived.

The sun in its near-winter low arc as it slid across the day variously shaded and highlighted the ravines and peaks of the Mt Hobson skyline.

The ideal situation is a dawn tie-up, and off again before dark. There is something almost hypnotic waiting for a vessel slowly, ever so slowly, to settle on its keel, and the longer wait for the tide to expose the prop and be shallow enough to stand and work on it. And then the process is reversed.

Waiting for the tide to ebb and flood induces hours of contemplation. As Melville said, 'meditation and water are wedded forever'. Being so aware of the movement of the sun and tide you get a powerful sense of nature's daily rhythm that normally goes unnoticed in our usual lives. There's a primeval simplicity and satisfaction that brings much greater reward than the frantic accumulation of possessions. And I always think of the grids at Duders, some 60 years ago.

Great Barrier – walking Port FitzRoy

Walking the many tracks about Port FitzRoy brings a sense of liberation. You will hardly ever meet anybody else, the landforms and the bush are awe inspiring, and the views from lookouts defy adequate description. It's like a walk back in time.

We like the walks across Kaikoura Island, even if the landscape, extensively farmed up until the 1970s, is now covered in rough scrub. The island is being allowed to regenerate naturally rather than be replanted. A lot of pinus radiata trees have been ring barked and are dying. Following a track along the hilltop grass airstrip eventually leads to Mt Overlook, and there you perch, right on the edge of a vertical cliff, 180 metres above the sea, looking northwards across Port Abercrombie and eastwards toward the wharf at Port FitzRoy. Walking in the opposite direction takes you along the ridge track, scrambling over volcanic outcrops to the westernmost end of the island, with unreal views over the Grey Group and Broken Islands and across to Little Barrier. This is one of the great profiles of Little Barrier – the folds of its mountains do indeed strikingly resemble, as the locals say, the image of a dead Queen Victoria lying on her bier. Europeans can also anthropomorphise a landscape.

Immediately behind the Port FitzRoy wharf are tracks which lead to volcanic abutments high above and overlooking the inlet.

But the more challenging walks are best accessed by boaties from Kaiarara Bay. Landing at Bush's Bay, just opposite Blair's Landing (now what a coincidence is this of modern war-mongers' names?), offers two routes to the summit of Mt Hobson.

The first, the Kaiarara Track, leads along the flats through the biggest nikau palms that I have ever seen, and across some of the coldest, stony streams, past the Kaiarara hut, and thence begins the ascent, gentle at first, through marvellous native bush. The well-formed track ever steepens, while ravines are effortlessly crossed by recent suspension bridges. The Department of Conservation has done the most amazing track work. Every now and then, through the dense bush, you can glimpse the towering, vertical volcanic escarpments immediately to the right.

Eventually you reach the short turnoff to where there were the remains of the old kauri log dam, built by George Murray in 1926. The massive storm of June 2014 wiped it off the face of the earth. We were shocked to read of the dam's demise for it was an amazing experience to see the scale and ingenuity of the kauri industry's engineers. Yet Great Barrier Island periodically experiences extremes of rainfall, and always has. In 1886, for example, the Kaiarara valley was hit by massive rainfall; the dams filled and overflowed in a matter of hours and had to be released urgently. Some 600 logs were lost out to sea beyond Port Abercrombie.[45] So much for claims that extreme weather is caused only by modern human activity.

Beyond that now ex-dam turnoff, the track gets seriously steep. The summit peak region is approached on an endless and gasp-inducing wooden stairway erected to protect the ground-nesting areas of the black petrels. There seem to be thousands of steps, some sections very steep, more like a ladder really. Eventually the small summit clearing with its trig station is reached, at 627 metres.

Visitor or intention books at such places are invariably filled with the most trite comments – 'awesome', 'wow', 'amazing'. But on one of our Mt Hobson climbs an inspired recent entry was apparently written by some rather scornful wife: 'Stewart's fucked!!!!' In our own breathless state we could just imagine poor Stewart tormented with unusual stress, presumably well out of his normal TV-couch comfort zone.

Each of the three times we have reached the summit, conditions have been different, ranging from 360 degrees of perfect visibility, to heavy cloud cover with brief glimpses of distant locations.

The descent is in some ways more painful than the ascent with knees unusually jarred by those vast numbers of wooden steps.

My favourite route to the summit is the South Track, which starts near the Kaiarara hut and consists of a very long uphill climb along a ridge before miraculously leveling out and traversing the side of the huge Hogs Back ridge. It seems so easy, and then you are at the new Mt Heale hut which is perched on the side of the mountain and looks west far across to Little Barrier, Mokohinau, Hen and Chickens and Poor Knights islands, and Bream Head. I'm not a fan for staying in Department of Conservation tramping huts, but with this view I could easily be tempted. The sense of an easy climb is then immediately destroyed, for just after crossing the base of the dramatic Mt Heale outcrop, wooden steps begin, parallel to those of the Kaiarara Track, and they seem even longer and steeper, if such were possible.

The third walk is far less stressful, though still long. Not far out from Bush's Bay the West Line Track leads to Forest Road, built by the Forest Service in the 1950s, leading eventually, before its descent towards Whangaparapara Harbour, to the sharp volcanic upthrust of Maungapiko, another classic Great Barrier Island lookout.

Each of these walks take some five or six hours return. Arriving back at the yacht in Kaiarara Bay is one of life's more sensual delights – a swim to cool and wash the sweaty body, a lazy attempt at fishing, a glass of wine and a sunset cockpit dinner, hopefully of snapper. Above, Mt Hobson slowly retreats into its evening shadows. A delicious tiredness takes over the body. Moreporks call to each other as the stars appear.

Great Barrier - Whangaparapara

Long before I knew anything much about Great Barrier Island I was aware of Whangaparapara Harbour since it was the supply port for the pirate radio station Radio Hauraki. Only my generation can understand the sense of excitement and liberation with the sudden onslaught of wall-to-wall rock music in 1966 after a young lifetime of the jaded and faded and outdated government-monopoly radio in New Zealand.

My admiration for the radio rebels has only deepened now that I am more familiar with the conditions they faced when anchored for broadcasting in the Colville Channel, just outside the three-mile territorial limit. Of course the DJs were all safe in Auckland, recording programmes that were broadcast a week later by the poor crew on their decrepit ship named *Tiri.* She was soon driven ashore in heavy weather at Whangaparapara, and her replacement, *Tiri II,* miraculously survived the very same fate. She was then blown right across the Gulf and beached at Uretiti in Northland. Against all odds the pirate radio station survived until a shore licence was finally granted in 1970. Ever since it gained legal respectability it's never had quite the same edge.

Sailing into Whangaparapara Harbour reveals what is the most jagged, sharp-toothed mountain skyline that I have ever seen in New Zealand. From the left looms the hulking Hogs Back, then at top centre the nippled peak of Hobson, dropping down to the right with the peaks of Mt Heale, then Mt Matawhero and other volcanic outcrops descending into the far right. I have spent an entire afternoon and evening anchored in the harbour photographing the rapidly changing patterns of light and shade projected across this craggiest of mountain backdrops by the declining sun.

Whangaparapara, now sleepy and abandoned to its surrounding bush-clad hills, was the noisy scene of industrial colonial extraction for a very long time. For almost a century, vast quantities of giant kauri logs came down a network of bullock tracks and tramways from the central mountains to be milled in the huge Kauri Timber Company yard in the harbour – claimed to be the largest mill in the southern hemisphere – or made into vast log rafts for towing to Auckland. The harbour was full of scows and other ships. A long wharf reached out to deep water. Old photographs show the scene wreathed in smoke and steam from all the heavy machinery.

Gold and silver were mined on nearby Mt Ahumata in the 1890s. The large derelict stamping battery still stands at Oroville, on the road going down to Whangaparapara. In the right conditions its banging could be heard on the Coromandel.

Activity in Whangaparapara had slowed by WWII, the last kauri stands pretty much depleted, the mines worked out or uneconomic.

In 1956 a whaling station was established and it initially caught about 100 humpback whales a year. But these numbers went into rapid decline, mainly because of intensified whaling in their tropical Pacific breeding grounds. The station closed in 1962.

Only a few bits of rusted machinery from the mill and the whaling station remain. Wharves and buildings have all been demolished. The bush from once-denuded hills has regrown. It is a quiet scene. The harbour is left to schools of dolphins and recreational boaties.

I love to anchor in Graveyard Bay, tucked just inside Lighthouse Point at the harbour entrance. That gives the best view of that stunning skyline, and across the harbour. It's a good spot to imagine a bustling, industrialised landscape complete with belching smoke, screaming saws and bustling tramways, followed later by thousands of wheeling seagulls and the sea stained with the blood of harpooned whales.

Great Barrier – former landscapes

As well as modern recreational wonders, the island offers fascinating landscapes of past human activity. Given the large land area and natural resources of Great Barrier, it has a long history of Maori occupation, first by Ngāi Tai, then domination by Ngāti Rehua of Ngāti Wai, with some presence and challenges by Marutūahu. Yet evidence suggests population sizes were relatively small compared to the size of the island.

Maori presence is not as immediately apparent as on other Gulf islands due to the heavy bush cover, yet archaeologists have recorded many hundreds of occupation sites throughout the island. Among the more specialised ones are stone working 'factories', perhaps most notably near obsidian deposits at Te Ahumata. Maori settlements were more common in coastal and lowland areas. Places like Kaikoura Island, for example, have many archaeological remains, as indeed do other sheltered coastal areas such as Katherine Bay, Whangaparapara, Okupu and Tryphena.

The young American William Webster claimed to have bought large areas of land bordering the Hauraki Gulf and Coromandel in the years 1836-39, including Great Barrier Island in 1838. He was financed by William Abercrombie and Jeremiah Nagle. The three claimed joint ownership of Great Barrier Island. Later, in 1844, when pre-1840 land claims were investigated, their landholding was reduced to the northern and western areas of the island, excluding a native reserve in Katherine Bay, which is still Maori-owned land.

Copper was discovered at Miners Cove in 1841 and the three men formed the Great Barrier Island Mining Company. They established a small settlement on the flat area near the copper deposit. The mine's first period of operation was 1842-45, and workers were sometimes transferred to Nagle Cove in Port Abercrombie where Nagle and Abercrombie were building what was then the biggest ship built in New Zealand. The *Stirlingshire* took seven years to build. She was a three-masted barque constructed with pohutukawa and kauri and was 33 metres in length. Launched in 1847, she was used mainly on the London-Hobart run.

There are contemporary sketches of the ship under construction in Nagle Cove. Today it is easy to see where it was built, on a small area of flat ground, snug amidst surrounding hillsides.

Mining stopped in 1845 but operated again 1851-58, this time under the ownership of the disruptive pair from the Kawau mine – Whitaker and Heale. During this time, Captain Ninnis, former manager of the Kawau mine, leased the Great Barrier mine for 12 months. The mine opened again with new owners in 1865 and operated until it closed again in 1868. There was no more commercial mining.

The mining settlement had a different character from that on Kawau. Mine workers were fewer, varying from 10 to 30, and their settlement was a temporary affair with a small number of houses that seem to have been removed each time the mine closed. It was a far less stable community than on Kawau, mostly itinerant miners and labourers, with little social infrastructure.

The mining itself was also quite different since tunneling was all above sea level and reached high and deep into the forbidding hillside of rugged Miners Point. Once the ore was dug out and released from high adits down wooden chutes to level ground it was crushed on the spot by a steam crusher, installed by Whitaker and Heale, loaded onto lighters and taken around to Katherine Bay for transfer to ships. Some ore was smelted at Kawau, but mostly it was packed into steel bins and shipped to England for smelting.

The mine was never a great commercial success. It produced less ore than its counterpart on Kawau, some 2500 tons.[46]

It seems few Maori were involved in any of this activity. Mining is not something that they were interested in, nor were they usually involved in any timber-sawing or building activity. It is claimed that they did drag the timber for the *Stirlingshire* out of the bush.

On my sea-kayak circumnavigation of the island I spent a day and a half at Miners Cove, sheltering from a gale south-westerly. The sky was cloudless, there was no shade and the temperature was in the high 20s. It was far too hot to take shelter in the tent, or even to pitch it during the day, so I made a blue polytarp sun shade and lay about for most of the time. I wanted to explore the flat area where mining buildings once were, but it is now dotted with flax bushes and covered in waist-high kikuyu, making it extremely difficult to walk, or rather crash, more than a few metres at a time. Apart from the blue-green stained mine entrance just above the high-tide mark at the end of the stony beach there are no immediate signs of any mining settlement. The hot wind roared off the sea and up the mountain valleys. It was a wild, barren spot. I was pleased to leave early one windless morning.

In the 1890s there was further mining on Great Barrier, for gold and silver, mostly near Mt Ahumata. It was not long lived.

The activity that most transformed the island was kauri extraction. Even by today's standards it was on a massive industrial scale, as it also was in other parts of northern New Zealand. Much of the existing indigenous forest on Great Barrier Island was either taken out for milling, or destroyed in the brutal process. Kauri timber felling began early in colonial times, but was seriously underway in the 1880s and continued until the accessible stands had been taken by the later 1930s.

Building dams to flush out the logs deposited in steep valley floors was a common technique. Many hundreds of dams were built in New Zealand. Kauri is a light, buoyant timber, suited to being sluiced down gullies. Dams might take many months to fill, depending on rainfall. When the dam doors swung open, logs were released in a giant torrent and ended up many kilometres away in the sea. In the Kaiarara valley there were seven dams in operation in the 1920s. These were often tripped in sequence to boost that massive thrust of water. There were claims that sometimes the thunderous roar of water and smashing logs could be heard in Auckland. Public excursions sometimes went out from Auckland to see the event. Large numbers of logs were often so badly damaged that they were not worth milling.

The steep Kaiarara valley was most suited to these driving dams. Elsewhere bullock teams transported the big logs, and then more serious mechanisation was developed using steam winches and steel cables. Logs were dragged up steep valley sides and tumbled down the other side, leaving a smashed, barren landscape.

The Kauri Timber Company eventually built a sophisticated tramway running some nine kilometres from the eastern slopes of Mt Hobson across the island to the mills at Whangaparapara. Winches and cables hauled logs placed on four-wheeled bogies up 10 inclines, some as steep as 45 degrees, with a total vertical distance of more than a kilometre. The downhill sections were fraught. Sometimes workers lay directly on the bogies beside the logs, leaning over and winding the brake drums directly onto the wheel rims. On flatter sections small steam locomotives, or lokeys as they were called, and rail tractors dragged the log trains. Paul Mahoney, the historian of New Zealand bush trams, argues that it was 'the most extraordinary forestry incline system built anywhere in the world'.[47] It operated from 1931 to 1940.

This route can be walked today. The Tramline Track, still with its straight, relentless inclines, stretches from Whangaparapara to meet Aotea Road due east of Mt Hobson.

Great Barrier – choices and challenges

The regeneration of the bush on Great Barrier Island has been a great success. Probably three-quarters or more of the island is now covered with greenery. In large part this has been natural regeneration, helped by the remarkable fact that the island has never had possums, wallabies, deer, ferrets, weasels, stoats or weka.

The former New Zealand Forest Service also planted some 150,000 kauri seedlings from the 1970s. Kauri grow quickly at first and there are many fine stands of young trees, especially in the Mt Hobson forest area.

On Kaikoura Island, now in public ownership and administered by the Motukaikoura Trust, wilding pines are being ring barked, and deer, pigs, rabbits and cats have been eradicated. Some private land owners have built predator fences to protect trees and birds, notably Glenfern, just opposite the Port FitzRoy wharf.

But there are problems. One of the great threats is the recent spread of the deadly kauri dieback disease, which is also affecting kauri on the mainland. This is caused by a fungus-like disease with microscopic spores that get into a tree's roots. It is thought that it can be spread by human shoes, hence the boot-spray and brush equipment at the start of many major tracks.

And while the island has a relatively limited range of predators – mainly ship rats, kiore, mice, wild pigs, cats and dogs – these still do major damage variously to plant, animal and birdlife. There is more birdlife than is usually seen on the mainland, but it is nothing like the variety or numbers seen on the predator-free islands. There are localised attempts at controlling these pests but there are no island-wide eradication programmes as yet.

Once when I camped at Akapoua Bay, in Port FitzRoy, I heard much scuffling in the night. I shone a torch through the tent insect mesh and there in the little vestibule were hundreds of pairs of black shiny eyes staring back at me. They were ship rats. I made a loud noise and they fled, but once the torch went out they rapidly sneaked back. After several of these episodes I left them alone to line up and stare at me in the dark, since they did not seem intent on chewing their way in, as has happened to us camped elsewhere in New Zealand.

In 2014 about half the land area of the island, and mostly in the northern regions, was declared Aotea Conservation Park. This may not provide complete protection since mining companies, for example, seem constantly alert to extracting more copper, gold and silver if the economics are ever in their favour, and if governments are keen to permit prospecting, as some are, even on conservation lands. 'No Mining' protest signs sometimes spring up around the island. It's a divisive issue for residents, some of whom are keen to see 'development' to provide employment, while others wish to retain a more pristine environment.

Another contentious issue is mussel farming. At present the four mussel farms inside Port FitzRoy do not inconvenience boaties too much, but if there are more of them the inland lake would quickly become a choked nightmare. You only have to look at the massive extent of these farms along the Coromandel west coast to see how environmentally and recreationally intrusive they can become.

Mussel farming (as well as oyster and salmon farming) has been a vexed political issue for some decades. Such was the big money demand for them that a government moratorium had to be implemented in 2002 to enable local authorities to sort out their policies. The legislative brakes are now off, yet so far Great Barrier Island has been spared further farms – but for how much longer? A massive expansion of oyster and mussel farms is proposed in the Firth of Thames.

Related issues have to do with whether local residents will have any say, or indeed employment, or whether the big companies will take over and operate mechanised rather than labour-intensive harvesting. In our observations over recent years much larger, noisier (and music-blasting) harvesting vessels, small ships rather than barges, seem to have taken over from smaller, local, outboard-powered mussel barges. The companies these days are more likely to be overseas owned rather than having local or even much New Zealand ownership.

With its clean, clear waters, Great Barrier Island will doubtless be a key aquaculture battleground in future struggles between environmentalists and corporate entities, as has already happened in places like Marlborough Sounds.

Having said all that, I have a sneaking admiration for mussel-farming skills. When they first started in New Zealand, in the 1970s, the technique was to have floating rafts with ropes trailing below to pick up natural spat and thus grow mussels. In more recent decades spat is gathered from drifting kelp on Ninety Mile Beach on the west coast. This spat is put into biodegradable endless stockings which are tied to loops of rope under row upon row of large plastic buoys. The spat attaches itself to the ropes, the stocking dissolves and the ropes are soon festooned with juicy, fat, green-lipped mussels, ready for harvesting inside two years.

Harvesting in Port FitzRoy creates a bit of a community stir. The locals all come out in their boats to fish close to the operating barges/vessels. The water is a dirty brown with all the residue stripped from the ropes and from the tumble washing of the mussels. Hundreds of damaged mussels go overboard during the sorting process, and the snapper go absolutely nuts underneath. If we had a freezer on board our yacht we could catch enough fish to last for months.

Marinas and moorings

Boating people are their own worst enemies. It's not their fault. It's the result of New Zealand's largest city being perched on the Hauraki Gulf, with its one and a half million citizens having the highest per capita rate of boat ownership of anywhere on the planet. The collective impact of recreational boating activity results in obvious pressure points – not only on fish and shellfish stocks but on the boating fraternity itself, especially with regard to marinas and moorings.

As yet there are no marinas on any of the Hauraki Gulf islands, and there probably will never be any on those islands that are Crown-owned reserves. However, there are no certainties. Mussel farms, for example, are leased areas of sea in Port FitzRoy surrounded by conservation land.

The politics of who or what actually administers and manages sea space as opposed to land space are very complex. There are often numerous and overlapping local authorities and jurisdictions. There is no uniform or national set of planning rules. It's all a bit of a mess.

More immediately, there is potential for marina building in suitable inlets in privately owned parts of Great Barrier, Kawau and Waiheke. Due to its population and proximity to Auckland, Waiheke is the first battleground with highly contested plans for a marina in Matiatia. Waiheke islanders are passionately divided over the issue. It's some comfort that the Environment Court threw out the developers' marina plans in December 2015. But pressure for a marina somewhere on Waiheke will not go away.

A greater concern for Hauraki Gulf boaties is the proliferation of moorings in some prime island bays that hinder or even preclude the chance of casual anchoring. The more notorious locations are North Cove and School House Bay on Kawau (and there are others on Kawau), Sandy Bay on Rakino and Matiatia on Waiheke. There has been a well-publicised and protracted legal wrangle over a single mooring in Woody Bay, Rakino, which illustrates the administrative and legal confusion and complexity. In this context it is not difficult for some naughty boat owners to establish illegal moorings and/or fail to comply with various requirements such as regular underwater inspections.

My general view is that whereas property rights are well entrenched for dry land, the sea should always remain public space and not be privatised – particularly not where there are pristine bays and inlets where lots of people go to enjoy themselves.

Exploiting and restoring islands

Today's sailors in the Hauraki Gulf are privileged to see the results of profound changes in values and attitudes towards most of its islands, especially those that are Crown reserves. Sitting in some wonderful evening anchorage, with a glass of wine, we can reflect on big themes that materialise before us, especially the shift from exploiting to restoring. And this is part of a related ethos already discussed – the early dispossession of the traditional owners and the attempts now at cultural and economic redress.

As we have seen, environmental damage all over New Zealand dates from the very first human settlement. The earliest Polynesian seafarers brought to New Zealand two mammals that became major predators – the Pacific rat (*Rattus exulans*) or kiore, and the dog or kuri. Both originally came from South-east Asia. Over the centuries, these two predators in combination with the economic activities of a growing Maori population resulted in mass bird extinctions, and extensive burning and clearing of the forests in lowland areas.

Dogs were valued for their meat, their skin and hair were used in clothing and decoration, they made great hunters, and they were good pets. They did not last long as a species after European contact since introduced dogs replaced them, mostly through interbreeding. Kiore were a food source for Maori. Though never domesticated, they were fed by Maori and they became part of their natural world. Ngāti Wai regard themselves even today as their guardians. Most kiore did not last long on the mainlands after European contact because they were no match for the newly introduced Norway and ship rats. They survived only in a few remote areas at the bottom of the South Island and on some offshore islands including many in the Hauraki Gulf

When the Department of Conservation began pest-eradication programmes to create predator-free islands in the Hauraki Gulf, there was an issue with Maori about poisoning kiore. The compromise was that the species would not be poisoned to extinction but, as mentioned earlier, it could continue to survive for scientific and cultural reasons on two islands – Mauitaha and Arāra in the western Chickens group of the Hen and Chickens Islands. Kiore are still widespread on Great Barrier Island.

The Hauraki Gulf islands, like the rest of New Zealand, came under more extreme environmental pressure with colonisation. A whole new range of predators scuttled ashore – such as ship rats, Norway rats, stoats, ferrets, weasels, wallabies, possums, deer, pigs, goats, rabbits, cats and dogs.

For almost the last 200 years, the islands were plundered for whatever economic resources they had – timber, copper, manganese, gold, silver, sand and shingle, basalt. They were farmed, denuded of native vegetation, and exotic trees and weeds were introduced. They were places to dump wrecked hulls, and rubbish from the city, and once there were plans to turn the closest island to the city, Browns Island, into a sewerage treatment plant.

When we moved into more ecologically and environmentally sensitive times, in the 1970s-80s, there began a momentum to try and restore, at least on some islands in New Zealand, a predator-free space and regenerating bush and have it as safe haven for a whole range of endangered native birds and insects.

Hauraki Gulf islands have significantly benefitted from this new attitude. Over the past 30 or so years, scientists with the Department of Conservation and committed groups of citizens have utterly transformed both key island landscapes and our appreciation of them. Rightly are they now referred to as Treasure Islands, and there has been huge public support.

Now many Gulf islands are well on the way to restoration. Many are now protected reserves. They are predator free, they have been replanted in native vegetation, and endangered native birds, insects and reptiles have been reintroduced. It's a wonderful story of our age.

Like most Aucklanders, I was aware of these programmes and

their success. But until I looked at the scientific literature and drew up predator eradication lists and tables for myself, I did not really appreciate the efforts and the technicalities of killing unwanted critters.[48] A simplified overview of pest eradication:

Little Barrier	cats 1977-80;
	kiore 2004
TiriTiri Matangi	kiore 1993
Mokohinau	kiore 1990-91
Hen Island (Taranga)	kiore 2011
Chicken Islands *	kiore 1994-97
Noisies – Maria/David	Norway rats 1959/61
Noisies – Otata/Motuhoropapa	Norway rats 1979-80, 2002
Rakino	Norway rats 2002
Motukawao	Norway rats 1977-79
Motutapu	possums/wallabies1990-97;
	cats/stoats/rabbits 2009-10
Rangitoto	possums/wallabies1990-97;
	cats/stoats/rabbits 2009-10
Motuihe	Norway rats/mice 1997;
	cats/rabbits 2005
Browns Island	rabbits 1985-91;
	Norway rats/mice 1995
Rotoroa	Norway rats/mice 2013
Pakatoa	Norway rats 2013

* Chicken Islands Mauitaha and Arāra have been left for kiore.

There have been localised attempts to reduce predators on Waiheke, Kawau and Great Barrier Island. Kaikoura Island on Great Barrier is a scenic reserve in public ownership and managed by a trust. It has been cleared of deer, pigs, rabbits and cats, with ship rats and kiore numbers kept in check. But that island's very close proximity to the main island of Great Barrier makes ship rat invasion an ongoing likelihood.

New Zealand scientists have been at the world's cutting edge of island pest eradication. Their efforts show a steep learning curve, not only with regard to experimental methods and quick adaptation to new poisons and technology, but also in better understanding the biological and social behaviour of the predators themselves.

Some of the earliest efforts were to remove Norway rats from various islands in the Noisies group. It was thought that only on small islands was eradication of rodents possible. First-generation baits were laid by hand, and seem to have been successful. But the eradication of Norway rats proved difficult due to their habit of reinvading by swimming from nearby Rakino, which is privately owned and was not initially targeted. Not until second-generation poisons were used on the Noisies and more especially on Rakino in 2002 could the Noisies be secured.

One of the most difficult of the early eradication tasks was getting rid of cats from Little Barrier in the late 1970s. Various techniques were used including different types of trapping (cage and leg hold), poisoning, shooting and dogs. The task was made especially difficult by the extremely rugged terrain and the requirement for large numbers of trap-baiting workers – almost 150, many of them volunteers – and thousands of person-days. And the cats were so cunning.

Eventually a total of 151 cats were destroyed, mostly by 1080 poison mixed with fish bait and leg-hold trapping. The dogs were useless.[49]

Pest eradication, particularly of rodents, was greatly advanced in the 1990s with the advent of second-generation anticoagulant poisons such as bromadiolone and, especially, brodifacoum. These chemicals are related to the common human blood anticoagulant medication called warfarin, but are much stronger. The newer anticoagulants make blood unable to clot and induce bleeding from small blood vessels. The internal bleeding causes shock, unconsciousness and death.

At the same time the use of helicopters for aerial dispersal of these poisons in pellet form became common, and good coverage on almost any terrain could be obtained by flying GPS grid patterns. But some ground-bait laying was generally used as a supplement, to help knock out any stray survivors and especially to try to prevent any reinvasion.

What had been unthinkable only a few years earlier was now possible, and on larger and larger islands in the Hauraki Gulf and elsewhere around New Zealand. Kiore, Norway rats, ship rats, mice, cats, possums, rabbits, as well as ferrets, stoats and weasels could be eradicated. According to D.R. Towns, 'By 2011, 147 populations of 13 species of vertebrates had been removed from at least 95 islands with a total area of 32,000ha.'[50]

One of the more interesting challenges, for the Hauraki Gulf, was the larger vertebrates on Rangitoto and Motutapu – the possums and wallabies. An initial aerial drop of 1080 poison in 1990 achieved a 93 per cent kill rate but it took eight years of hard ground work to remove the remainder by trapping, cyanide poisoning, spotlight shooting and use of dogs. In all some 21,000 possums and 12,500 wallabies were destroyed. More than a decade later, these two islands were cleared of cats, stoats and rabbits with an aerial drop of brodifacoum.[51]

Pest eradication in the Hauraki Gulf islands, and elsewhere in New Zealand, has been an unprecedented success story, and is an enviable international example.[52]

Yet the process remains somewhat fraught on several fronts.

There has to be constant monitoring and bait-station efficiency at all times to prevent unwanted predators from returning, particularly off recreational boats. There are occasional scares, for example a recent one on Motuora, when a stray rodent was spotted. These scares require immediate and expensive efforts to capture the animal, mostly with extra poison bait-stations and traps. The best trap bait seems to be peanut butter.

Once we were walking to the summit of Rangitoto when around the corner came a man with a gun and a dog – a rather disturbing sight. He turned out not to be a killer on the loose but was following up a highly dubious rumour of a cat spotted on the island. His dog had neat little leather boots to help it on the razor sharp lava. But looking at our armed hunter gazing wistfully over the vast expanse of impossibly twisted rock it seemed like an exercise in futility.

The issue of poisoning, and especially aerial poison drops, inevitably upsets small but very vocal sections of the community who argue that it is a dangerous act. This takes the argument into the political arena and conservationists can never assume that their views will prevail. The major predator-removal programmes on Hauraki Gulf islands have been those controlled by the Department of Conservation and are on largely uninhabited islands.

Saturation aerial-poison drops in inhabited places such as Kawau, Waiheke and Great Barrier Island are unlikely to ever happen. Even the most cautiously planned and limited efforts at ground-based rodent eradication, or even discussion of such a possibility, generates some vocal community opposition, as is happening on Kawau and Great Barrier Island.[53]

And there are other issues too. Mass poisoning does kill some non-target species, such as some native birds. Fortunately, numbers are relatively small – so the benefits far exceed this disadvantage. One exception seems to be the poor pukeko, which peck at poison pellets or dead predators, yet fortunately they are not an endangered species, if anything the reverse is the case. The poisoning of kiore on Tiritiri Matangi caused a 90 per cent decline in the pukeko population, yet within two years they were back to their pre-poison numbers.[54]

The Department of Conservation sometimes culls pukeko on the reservation islands because of their prolific breeding, the fact that they are destructive of young native vegetation (especially newly planted trees and shrubs), and their habit of attacking the young of other native birds. Later in 2015 there was a disastrous consequence when amateur hunters engaged by the Department to cull pukeko on Motutapu somehow ended up shooting four takahe. That's one fifth of the takahe population on the island, not to mention that takahe are among the most endangered bird species on earth with only about 300 remaining. Nobody was impressed.

Finally, nothing happens without a consequence. Creating a predator-free island sometimes means that various introduced weed species that have been kept in check by the predators now flourish and become a significant invasive problem. Considerable effort and expense is now required to spot and deal with these weeds.

Alas, there is no perfect status quo.

Exploiting and not restoring the sea

If islands restoration has been a great success story, the same cannot be said of the seas that surround them. The waters of the Hauraki Gulf look magnificent, but all is far from well, in fact we are quite some way down the road to ecological crisis. There may be arguments as to exactly how bad things are, but there is no argument that things are getting progressively worse rather than better.

The Hauraki Gulf Marine Park Act (2000) requires the Hauraki Gulf Forum to publish a detailed account of the Hauraki Gulf every three years. The *State of Our Gulf* reports are beautifully produced documents and contain a mass of scientific information. The reports for 2008, 2011 and 2014 can also be downloaded for free from the

Auckland Council website.

The tragedy is that nothing serious is ever done to try to change the environmental degradation. There's plenty of talk. But no action. Vested commercial interests and selfish recreational groups always hold sway.

The 2014 report also has a separate and very brief 'popular summary' (also downloadable) which encapsulates the key issues. It should be compulsory reading for everyone who goes boating in Auckland. Its conclusion is stark: 'the cumulative impact of all activities is still pointing towards the suppression of environmental values at low levels, and progressive environmental decline …'. It highlights the decline in fish stocks, especially snapper which are 'well below the level for maximum sustainable yield'. Shellfish in coastal areas have long been decimated by recreational gatherers and, in the inner Gulf, by commercial dredging. And now commercial dredging of scallops in the outer Gulf is depleting these stocks and further destroying the seabed.

Nitrogen loads from intensive dairy farming on the Hauraki Plains cause raised carbon dioxide levels and reduced oxygen levels and acidification. These effects are most marked in the Firth of Thames, ironically the location of major mussel and oyster farms (and many more are proposed for there).

Also pouring out of the Hauraki Plains' Waihou and Piako rivers is a vast quantity of sediment that also affects the Firth and the whole of the inner Hauraki Gulf. 'Three quarters of monitored Auckland water quality sites showed deteriorating trends in total suspended solids between 2004 and 2013,' the Hauraki Gulf Forum report says. This has serious consequences for a vast array of marine life. It also causes the current rapid invasion of mangroves all around the Gulf tidal coastlines and estuaries. Then there are problems with heavy metals such as copper, lead and zinc, most notably in urban estuaries and in the south eastern Firth of Thames.

Marine invasive species continue to arrive, four new species since 2011 including the serious Mediterranean fanworm. Bryde's whales are being killed by ships faster than their breeding rate. Seabirds such as the endemic black petrel and the fleshfooted shearwater are in decline due to commercial long-line fishing. Of course that exponential growth and expansion of suburban Auckland along hitherto largely unsettled Gulf coastlines only adds to the environmental pressures.

It's all a bit depressing.

There is one, albeit tiny, bright spot. Before commercial mussel dredging, vast areas of the Hauraki Gulf seabed were covered in millions of mussels providing filtering of water sediments and a habitat for fish and crustaceans. Starting in 1910 the whole of the inner Hauraki Gulf seabed from the Waitemata Harbour across to the Coromandel was dredged. By the 1960s this industry predictably collapsed, leaving a sea floor of bare sediment, an underwater desert. The same is now happening with commercial dredging of deep-water scallops, while in inshore waters recreational fishermen with their cheap dredges from the Warehouse are adding to the havoc on the seabed.

In 2012 the Mussel Reef Restoration Trust was formed and some test areas of the Gulf are being 'replanted' with undersize mussels from the commercial industry. Early results are promising. It seems that grown mussels can live and reproduce on a barren sea floor, but mussel spat will not take hold by itself on bare sediment. Many tonnes of adult mussels are currently being tipped into selected areas. The organisers are hoping at some stage to buy an existing mussel farm to ensure adequate supplies of mussels for extensive seeding.

If significant areas of the Gulf seabed were to become covered in mussels again, they would have to be protected somehow; otherwise a few boats with a dredge could readily clean them out.

Just as islands are best restored and protected by government reservation status, so the sea requires no-go fishing and dredging areas – that is, marine reserves. It is a national disgrace that only 0.3 per cent of Hauraki Gulf waters are in a marine reserve – the original reserve at Goat Island, as well as small ones at Okura-Long Bay, Te

Matuku on Waiheke, Tawharanui, and Motu Manawa-Pollen Island in the upper Waitemata Harbour.

While everybody knows how these tiny areas are hugely successful in protecting and restoring marine life, both the commercial and the recreational fishing lobbies always defeat attempts to create any substantial marine reserves that would actually make a serious difference to overall fish stocks in the Gulf. Some Maori groups too, including Ngāti Wai, are also opposed to creating more marine reserves, arguing that denies them traditional fishing rights claimed under the Treaty of Waitangi.

The more selfish humans are in these matters, the more they eventually defeat their own longer-term interests.

There are occasional government mutterings about ending commercial fishing in the Hauraki Gulf, but I'll believe it when it happens. The long history of overfishing the Gulf, and the failure to create substantial marine reserves, is unlikely to stop anytime soon.

But even if such reserves could magically be created, there is that major problem with declining water quality due to agricultural runoff and sediment build up. How that might be mitigated is a major political question, and one that no government wants to address seriously. Again, talk, but little action.

But there is a problem that we all have. The Hauraki Gulf affords us with relatively good fishing (even if not what it once was), and away from the harbour we can safely gather mussels and oysters. It's a recreationally happy place, and the scenery is stunning. Many tens of thousands of us love the Gulf. Mostly we can't immediately see the marine degradation. It is not easy to get our heads around the fact that the waters are not in good shape, and are getting worse. Perhaps we don't really want to.

End of the day

So much about sailing involves routine activities, most of which are not only necessary tasks but also comforting rituals. The most pleasing for me are those towards the end of a summer day when cosily anchored in a quiet spot. An early-evening fish in the hope of a fresh meal, a glass or two of red wine, and the cooking of dinner whether it be fresh fish or something else from a packet or can. Then doing the dishes and having a cup of tea.

As the sun goes down maybe another attempt at fishing, this time for mackerel to be salted for tomorrow's fishing. Merrilyn is the master mackerel catcher.

A walk around the deck, checking the sail cover and tightening any halyards that might bang in the night. A quick pull at each of the shrouds to make sure nothing is amiss. A check too on the anchor rode – a good angle and properly fastened? Making sure the dinghy drogue is clipped on and the painter is secure. Then hooking up the cabin top anchor light. Fitting the mosquito net across the open cabin entrance, and another over the forward hatch opening.

A lingering look at the darkening world and the quickly brightening stars. Time to fluff up the sleeping bags, sometimes a quick read, then lights out. Morepork call.

I have a sense of utter belonging and contentment. A journey has been completed – or, as sailors say, a passage made.

I'm asleep on a boat way out beyond Rangitoto.

Thanks to

- my parents who gave me a carefree childhood on beaches and little boats.
- Merrilyn for sharing Gulf explorations.
- Paul Monin and Russell Stone for their outstanding historical research on the Hauraki Gulf. I have relied heavily on their work. Paul Monin also kindly read the manuscript and offered much appreciated advice and support.
- Mike Lee for reading the manuscript and making detailed comments and corrections.
- Geoff Walker for providing editorial and publishing advice.
- Bruce Hayward for answering some of my naïve geological questions.
- Peter McBurney for providing a copy of his marvellous research paper 'Traditional History Overview of the Mahurangi and Gulf Islands Districts'.
- Beth Reynolds of the Department of Conservation for providing a hard-to-get copy of Brenda Sewell, *The History and Archaeology of the Coppermine at Miners Head.*
- all those government and private organisations and volunteers who have prevented rampant commercial development, killed predators, planted trees, reintroduced endangered species and created Auckland's greatest asset – the Treasure Islands.

References

1 K.R. Howe, *Coastal Sea Kayaking in New Zealand. A practical touring manual,* Auckland, 2005.

2 Paul Monin, *Waiheke Island. A history*, Palmerston North, 1992, p.26.

3 Paul Monin, *Matiatia. Gateway to Waiheke*, Wellington, 2012, p.108.

4 K.R. Howe, *Nature, Culture and History. The 'Knowing' of Oceania,* Honolulu, 2000.

5 Peter McBurney, 'Traditional History Overview of the Mahurangi and Gulf Islands Districts', research report commissioned by the Mahurangi and Gulf Islands Districts Collective Committee in association with the Crown Forestry Rental Trust, Wai 1040 A36, Te Paparahi o Te Raki (Northland) inquiry, 2010, p.7.

6 McBurney, p.9.

7 Taimoana Tūroa, *Te Takoto o te Whenua o Hauraki. Hauraki landmarks,* (ed) Te Ahukaramū Charles Royal, Auckland, 2000, pp.110-111.

8 The best detailed accounts of Maori 'political' history of the region can be found in the listed works of Paul Monin and Russell Stone. Additional valuable material comes from Peter McBurney, Barry Rigby, Charles Royal, Taimoana Tūroa, Rāwiri Taonui.

9 Olive Wright, *New Zealand 1826-1827 from the French of Dumont D'Urville,* Wellington, 1950, pp.222-223.

10 Wright, pp.152,156.

11 *NZ Herald*, 16 Feb 1903, Papers Past.

12 Janet Davidson, 'Archaeological excavations at the Station Bay pa, Motutapu Island, inner Hauraki Gulf, New Zealand', *Tuhinga,* 24, Te Papa Museum, 2013, pp.5-47.

13 Davidson, p.40.

14 *NZ Herald,* 7 Mar 2014.

15 K.R. Howe, *Nature, Culture and History. The 'Knowing' of Oceania,* Honolulu, 2000.

16 Helen Beaglehole, *Always the Sound of the Sea. The daily lives of New Zealand's lighthouse keepers*, Nelson, 2009, p.199.

17 Andy Dodd, 'Tiritiri Matangi Archaeological and Historic Landscape. Heritage Assessment', Department of Conservation, 2008.

18 Nigel Prickett, 'An archaeological survey of the Chickens Islands (Marotere), New Zealand, *Tane*, 30, 1984, pp.177-197; Bruce Hayward, P.R. Moore and Mary Newman, 'Archaeological site survey of Hen Island (Taranga)', *Tane*, 24, 1978, pp.137-157.

19 P.R. Moore, 'Mineral exploration on Coppermine Island 1849-1969: an historical review', *Tane,* 30, 1984, pp.165-175.

20 Good overviews of Maori fishing are Janet Davidson, *The Prehistory of New Zealand,* Auckland, 1984; Chris D. Paulin, 'Perspectives of Maori fishing history and

techniques. Ngā āhua me ngā pūrākau me ngā hangarau ika o te Māori', *Tuhinga* 18, 2007, pp.11–47.

21 G.E. Machovsky-Capuska, 'Hunting between the air and the water. The Australasian gannet (*Morus serrator*)', PhD thesis in Ecology, Massey University, 2012.

22 New Zealand Birds Online: http://nzbirdsonline.org.nz/

23 Helen Beaglehole, *Always the Sound of the Sea. The daily lives of New Zealand's lighthouse keepers*, Nelson, 2009, p.59.

24 Duncan M. Cunningham, and Philip J. Moors, 'The birds of the Noises [sic] Islands, Hauraki Gulf', *Notornis. Journal of the Ornithological Society of New Zealand,* 32:3, 1985, pp.221-243.

25 J.W.B MacKay, and J.C. Russell, S.H. Anderson, 'Birds of Motuhoropapa I, Noises [sic] Group, Hauraki Gulf, North Is, New Zealand', *Notornis,* Vol. 54, 2007, pp.197-200.

26 *Scoop*, 20 Oct 2005.

27 D.M. Stafford, *Te Arawa. A history of the Arawa people*, Auckland, 1967, p.17.

28 Michael Lee, 'Biota of seven islets off Waiheke Island, inner Hauraki Gulf', *Tane,* 37, 1999, pp.99-136.

29 *New Zealand Herald*, 8 January 2001.

30 Useful sources on the copper mine are Kenneth Brown, 'Halfway round the world and back: The most travelled Cornish pumping engine. The story of a New Zealand copper mining fiasco': http://www.aditnow.co.uk/documents/Kawau-Island-Copper-Mine-Copper-Mine/Kawau-Mine.pdf
Rod Clough, 'The archaeology of the historic copper industry on Kawau Island, 1843-1855, 1899-1901', *Australasian Historical Archaeology*, 9, 1991, pp.45-48; Ken Pointin, 'Island pump house. Early copper mining on Kawau Island': http:/www.motatsociety.org.nz/The_Driving.../Island%20Pumphouse.pdf

31 A Voyager, *Daily Southern Cross,* 28 May 1852, p.4, Papers Past.

32 Mark Hickford, 'Settling some very important principles of colonial law. Three "forgotten" cases of the 1840s', *Victoria University of Wellington Law Review*, 35, 2004, pp.1-30.

33 A good overview is Department of Conservation, *Kawau Island Historic Reserve. Hauraki Gulf Marine Park*, Auckland, 2007.

34 J.A. Froude, *Oceana, or, England and Her Colonies*, London, 1886, p.195.

35 Useful sources on wallabies are Pohutukawa Trust New Zealand: http://www.pohutukawatrust.org.nz/index.htm
National Possum Control Agencies, *Pest Wallabies. Control and monitoring of pest Dama and Bennett's Wallabies*, A9, June 2007; W.B. Shaw, and R.J. Pierce, *Management of North Island weka and wallabies on Kawau Island,* Department of Conservation Science Internal Series 54, Department of Conservation, July 2002; Colin Bright, 'Some facts about the Wallabies on Kawau Island', April 2009: www.

kawauisland.org.nz/downloads/wallabyFacts.pdf

36 Paul Quinlan Landscape Architect Ltd, 'Kawau Island Historic Reserve Pine Forest Harvesting Proposal Visual & Landscape Assessment', draft, 11 April 2014: http://www.doc.govt.nz/Documents/getting-involved/consultations/2014/kawau-island/visual-landscape-assessment-11-04-14-draft.pdf

37 Harry Bioletti, 'Place names of Kawau Island and the Mahurangi Harbour', MA Thesis, University of Auckland, 1985, pp.130-131.

38 Wright, p.157.

39 John Logan Campbell, *Poenamo Revisited. A facsimile of the 1898 edition of Poenamo by Sir John Logan Campbell,* Essay and notes by R.C.J. Stone, Auckland, 2012, p.20.

40 Campbell, p.308.

41 Campbell, p.308.

42 Paul Monin, *Hauraki Contested 1769-1875*, Wellington, 2001, chapter 5; Monin,, 'Maori economies and colonial capitalism', in Giselle Byrnes (ed), *The New Oxford History of New Zealand*, Melbourne, 2009, pp.125-146; Andy Dodd, 'Motukorea/Browns Island Archaeological Landscape Heritage Assessment', Department of Conservation, 2006.

43 Information from Mike Lee.

44 Paul Monin, 'The islands lying between Slipper Island in the south-east, Great Barrier Island in the north and Tiritiri-Matangi in the north-west', Report for Waitangi Tribunal, 1996.

45 *NZ Herald,* 13 April 1886, Papers Past.

46 Brenda Sewell, *The History and Archaeology of the Coppermine at Miners Head, Great Barrier Island*, Auckland, 1999.

47 Paul Mahoney *The Era of the Bush Tram in New Zealand*, Wellington, 2004, p.16.

48 Among the more useful sources are M.N. Clout, and J.C. Russell, 'The eradication of mammals from New Zealand islands', in Koike, F., M., Clout, et al. (eds.), *Assessment and Control of Biological Invasion Risks*, Kyoto, 2006, pp.127-141; C.R. Veitch, and M.N. Clout (eds), *Turning the Tide. The eradication of invasive species,* Proceedings of the International Conference on eradication of island invasives, Cambridge, 2002; C.R. Veitch, M.N. Clout and D.R. Towns (eds), *Island Invasives. Eradications and management,* Auckland, 2011.

49 C.R. Veitch, C.R. 'The eradication of feral cats (*Felis catus*) from Little Barrier Island, New Zealand', *New Zealand Journal of Zoology*, 28:1, 2001, pp.1-12.

50 D.R. Towns, 'Eradications of invertebrate pests from islands around New Zealand. What have we delivered and what have we learned?', in Veitch, Clout and Towns, p.364.

51 S.C. Mowbray, 'Eradication of introduced Australian marsupials (brushtail possum and brushtail rock wallaby) from Rangitoto and Motutapu Islands, New Zealand', in Veitch and Clout, pp.226-232.

52 C.R. Veitch, and M.N. Clout (eds), *Turning the Tide. The eradication of invasive*

species, Proceedings of the International Conference on eradication of island invasives, Cambridge, 2002; C.R. Veitch, M.N. Clout and D.R. Towns (eds), *Island Invasives. Eradications and management,* Auckland, 2011.

53 J. Ogden, J., and J. Gilbert, 'Running the gauntlet. Advocating rat and feral cat eradication on an inhabited island – Great Barrier Island, New Zealand', in Veitch, Clout and Towns, pp.467-471.

54 C.R. Veitch, 'Eradication of Pacific rats (*Rattus exulans*) from Tiritiri Matangi island, Hauraki Gulf, New Zealand', in Veitch and Clout, pp.360-364; J.E. Dowding, E.C. Murphy and C.R. Veitch, 'Brodifacoum residues in target and non-target species following an aerial poisoning operation on Motuihe Island, Hauraki Gulf, New Zealand', *New Zealand Journal of Ecology,* 23:2, 1999, pp.207-214.

Bibliography

Armitage, Don, Great Barrier Island history website: https://sites.google.com/a/aotea.org/don-armitage/Home

A Voyager, 'A cruise in the Gulf of Houraki', *Daily Southern Cross*, 28 May, 1852, p.4, Papers Past.

Balderston, David, *The Waiheke Ferries of Auckland*, Wellington, 1991.

Ballara, Angela, *Taua. 'Musket wars', 'land wars', or tikanga? Warfare in Maori society in the early nineteenth century*, Auckland, 2003.

Beaglehole, Helen, *Lighting the Coast. A history of New Zealand's coastal lighthouse system*, Christchurch, 2006.

Beaglehole, Helen, *Always the Sound of the Sea. The daily lives of New Zealand's lighthouse keepers*, Nelson, 2009.

Bercusson, Linda, and John Walsby, *Exploring the Hauraki Gulf. From Bream Head to the Coromandel*, Nelson, 2008.

Bioletti, Harry, 'Place names of Kawau Island and the Mahurangi Harbour', MA Thesis, University of Auckland, 1985.

Bright, Colin, 'Some facts about the Wallabies on Kawau Island', April 2009: www.kawauisland.org.nz/downloads/wallabyFacts.pdf

Brown, Kenneth, 'Halfway round the world and back: The most travelled Cornish pumping engine. The story of a New Zealand copper mining fiasco': http://www.aditnow.co.uk/documents/Kawau-Island-Copper-Mine-Copper-Mine/Kawau-Mine.pdf

Campbell, John Logan, *Poenamo Revisited. A facsimile of the 1898 edition of Poenamo by Sir John Logan Campbell*, Essay and notes by R.C.J. Stone, Auckland, 2012.

Clough, Rod, 'The archaeology of the historic copper industry on Kawau Island, 1843-1855, 1899-1901', *Australasian Historical Archaeology*, 9, 1991, pp.45-48.

Clout, M.N. and J.C. Russell, 'The eradication of mammals from New Zealand islands', in Koike, F., M., Clout, et al. (eds.), *Assessment and Control of Biological Invasion Risks*, Kyoto, 2006, pp.127-141.

Corbett, Peter D., *A First Class Defended Port. The history of the coast defences of Auckland, its harbour and approaches*, Auckland, 2003.

Cunningham, Duncan M. and Philip J. Moors, 'The birds of the Noises [sic] Islands, Hauraki Gulf', *Notornis. Journal of the Ornithological Society of New Zealand*, 32:3, 1985, pp.221-243.

Diamond, J.T., and B.W. Hayward, *Kauri Timber Dams*, Auckland, n.d.

Davidson, Janet, *The Prehistory of New Zealand*, Auckland, 1984.

Davidson, Janet, 'Archaeological excavations at the Station Bay pa, Motutapu Island, inner Hauraki Gulf, New Zealand', *Tuhinga*, 24, Te Papa Museum, 2013, pp.5-47.

Department of Conservation website: http://www.doc.govt.nz/

Department of Conservation, *Kawau Island Historic Reserve. Hauraki Gulf Marine Park*, Auckland, 2007.

Dodd, Andy, 'Motuihe Quarantine Station (1870-1930), HMNZS *Tamaki* (1941-1963)', Heritage Assessment, Department of Conservation, 2006.

Dodd, Andy, 'Motukorea/Browns Island Archaeological Landscape Heritage Assessment', Department of Conservation, 2006.

Dodd, Andy, 'Te Maraeroa Flat, Little Barrier Island. Heritage Assessment', Department of Conservation, 2007.

Dodd, Andy, 'S.S. *Wairarapa* Graves, 1894. Heritage Assessment', Department of Conservation, 2007.

Dodd, Andy, 'Tiritiri Matangi Archaeological and Historic Landscape. Heritage Assessment', Department of Conservation, 2008.

Dodd, Andy, 'Motutapu Archaeological and Historic Landscapes. Heritage Assessment', Department of Conservation, 2008.

Dowding, J.E, E.C. Murphy and C.R. Veitch, 'Brodifacoum residues in target and non-target species following an aerial poisoning operation on Motuihe Island, Hauraki Gulf, New Zealand', *New Zealand Journal of Ecology*, 23:2, 1999, pp.207-214.

Duder, Tessa, *Night Race to Kawau*, Auckland, 1982.

Elliot, Molly G., *Island on the Skyline. Great Barrier Island*, Auckland, 1971.

Froude, J.A., *Oceana, or, England and Her Colonies*, London, 1886.

Hauraki Gulf Marine Park Board, *The Story of the Hauraki Gulf*, Auckland, 1983.

Hauraki Gulf Forum, *State of Our Gulf. Tikapa Moana – Hauraki Gulf state of the environment report 2011*, Auckland, 2011.

Hauraki Gulf Forum, *State of Our Gulf 2014. Tikapa Moana/Te Moananui a Toi. State of the environment report 2014*, Auckland, 2014.

Hauraki Gulf Forum, *State of Our Gulf. Popular summary*, Auckland, 2014.

Hayward, Bruce W., P.R. Moore and Mary Newman, 'Archaeological site survey of Hen Island (Taranga)', *Tane*, 24, 1978, pp.137-157.

Hayward, Bruce W., Graeme Murdoch and Gordon Maitland, *Volcanoes of Auckland. The essential guide*, Auckland, 2011.

Hickford, Mark, 'Settling some very important principles of colonial law. Three "forgotten" cases of the 1840s', *Victoria University of Wellington Law Review*, 35, 2004, pp.1-30.

Howe, K.R., *Nature, Culture and History. The 'Knowing' of Oceania,* Honolulu, 2000.

Howe, K.R., *The Quest for Origins. Who first discovered and settled New Zealand and the Pacific Islands?,* Auckland, 2003.

Howe, K.R. (ed), *Vaka Moana. Voyages of the ancestors. The discovery and settlement of the Pacific,* Auckland, 2006.

Howe, K.R., *Coastal Sea Kayaking in New Zealand. A practical touring manual,* Auckland, 2005.

Leach, Helen, *1000 Years of Gardening in New Zealand,* Wellington, 1984.

Lee, Michael, 'Biota of seven islets off Waiheke Island, inner Hauraki Gulf', *Tane,* 37, 1999, pp.99-136.

Locker, R.H., *Jade River. A history of the Mahurangi,* Warkworth, 2001.

Maddock, Shirley, and Don Whyte, *Islands of the Gulf,* Auckland, 1966.

Mahoney, Paul, *The Era of the Bush Tram in New Zealand,* Wellington, 2004.

McBurney, Peter, 'Traditional History Overview of the Mahurangi and Gulf Islands Districts', research report commissioned by the Mahurangi and Gulf Islands Districts Collective Committee in association with the Crown Forestry Rental Trust, Wai 1040 A36, Te Paparahi o Te Raki (Northland) inquiry, 2010.

McCormick, Herb, *As Long as it's Fun. The epic voyages and extraordinary times of Lin and Larry Pardey,* Arcata, Ca., 2014.

MacKay, J.W.B, and J.C. Russell, S.H. Anderson, 'Birds of Motuhoropapa I, Noises [sic] Group, Hauraki Gulf, North Is, New Zealand', *Notornis,* Vol. 54, 2007, pp.197-200.

Machovsky-Capuska, G.E., 'Hunting between the air and the water. The Australasian gannet (*Morus serrator*)', PhD thesis in Ecology, Massey University, 2012.

Maritime New Zealand, lighthouse information: http://www.maritimenz.govt.nz/Commercial/Shipping-safety/Aids-to-navigation/Lighthouses-of-New-Zealand.asp

Mitcalfe, Barry, *Gulf,* Coromandel, 1980.

Monin, Paul, *Waiheke Island. A history,* Palmerston North, 1992.

Monin, Paul, 'The islands lying between Slipper Island in the south-east, Great Barrier Island in the north and Tiritiri-Matangi in the north-west', Report for Waitangi Tribunal, 1996.

Monin, Paul *Hauraki Contested 1769-1875,* Wellington, 2001.

Monin, Paul, 'Maori economies and colonial capitalism', in Giselle Byrnes (ed),

The New Oxford History of New Zealand, Melbourne, 2009, pp.125-146.

Monin, Paul, *Matiatia. Gateway to Waiheke*, Wellington, 2012.

Moore, P.R., 'Mineral exploration on Coppermine Island 1849-1969: an historical review', *Tane*, 30, 1984, pp.165-175.

Mowbray, S.C., 'Eradication of introduced Australian marsupials (brushtail possum and brushtail rock wallaby) from Rangitoto and Motutapu Islands, New Zealand', in Veitch and Clout, pp.226-232.

Mussel 'magic carpet' for Hauraki Gulf: http://www.nzherald.co.nz/element-magazine/news/article.cfm?c_id=1503340&objectid=11324593

Mussel Reef Restoration Trust: http://reviveourgulf.org.nz/about.html

National Possum Control Agencies, *Pest Wallabies. Control and monitoring of pest Dama and Bennett's Wallabies*, A9, June 2007.

New Zealand Birds Online: http://nzbirdsonline.org.nz/

Office of Treaty Settlements: http://nz01.terabyte.co.nz/ots/OTShome.asp

Ogden, J., and J. Gilbert, 'Running the gauntlet. Advocating rat and feral cat eradication on an inhabited island – Great Barrier Island, New Zealand', in Veitch, Clout and Towns, pp.467-471.

Owen, William, *The Hauraki Gulf. A fishing and cruising guide*, Auckland, 1983.

Papers Past: http://paperspast.natlib.govt.nz/cgi-bin/paperspast

Pardey, Larry, *Details of Classical Boat Construction: the hull*, New York, 1991.

Pardey, Lin, *Bull Canyon. A boat builder, a writer and other wildlife*, Arcata, Ca., 2011.

Parson, Daryl, 'Green-lipped mussels and the Hauraki Gulf': http://www.aucklandcouncil.govt.nz/EN/AboutCouncil/representativesbodies/haurakigulfforum/Documents/GreenlippedmusselsandtheHaurakiGulfDarrenParsons.pdf

Paul Quinlan Landscape Architect Ltd, 'Kawau Island Historic Reserve Pine Forest Harvesting Proposal Visual & Landscape Assessment', draft, 11 April 2014: http://www.doc.govt.nz/Documents/getting-involved/consultations/2014/kawau-island/visual-landscape-assessment-11-04-14-draft.pdf

Paulin, Chris D., 'Perspectives of Maori fishing history and techniques. Ngā āhua me ngā pūrākau me ngā hangarau ika o te Māori', *Tuhinga* 18, 2007, pp.11–47.

Phillips, F.L., *Nga Tohu a Tainui. Landmarks of Tainui*, Otorohanga, vol 1, 1989.

Pohutukawa Trust New Zealand: http://www.pohutukawatrust.org.nz/index.htm

Pointin, Ken, 'Island pump house. Early copper mining on Kawau Island': http:/www.motatsociety.org.nz/The_Driving.../Island%20Pumphouse.pdf

Prickett, Nigel, 'An archaeological survey of the Chickens Islands (Marotere),

New Zealand, *Tane*, 30, 1984, pp.177-197.

Rigby, Barry, 'The Crown, Maori, and Mahurangi, 1840-1881. A historical report commissioned by the Waitangi Tribunal', 1998.

Riley, Murdoch, *Maori Bird Lore. An introduction,* Paraparaumu, 2001.

Rimmer, Anne, *Tiritiri Matangi. A model of conservation, Auckland, 2004.*

Robinson, Ian D., *Hauraki Gulf,* Auckland, 2008.

Royal, Te Ahukaramū Charles, 'Hauraki tribes', *Te Ara. The Encyclopedia of New Zealand*, updated 25 Mar 2014: http://www.TeAra.govt.nz/en/hauraki-tribes

Royal, Te Ahukaramū Charles, 'Marutūahu tribes', *Te Ara. The Encyclopedia of New Zealand*, updated 9 Nov 2012: http://www.TeAra.govt.nz/en/marutuahu-tribes

Sewell, Brenda, *The History and Archaeology of the Coppermine at Miners Head, Great Barrier Island*, Auckland, 1999.

Shaw, W.B., and R.J. Pierce, *Management of North Island weka and wallabies on Kawau Island,* Department of Conservation Science Internal Series 54, Department of Conservation, July 2002.

Sobel, Dava, *Longitude*, London, 1995.

Stafford, D.M., *Te Arawa. A history of the Arawa people*, Auckland, 1967.

Stone, R.C.J., *From Tamaki-Makau-Rau to Auckland*, Auckland, 2001.

Taonui, Rāwiri, 'Tāmaki tribes', *Te Ara. The Encyclopedia of New Zealand*, updated 4 Dec 2012: http://www.TeAra.govt.nz/en/tamaki-tribes

Taonui, Rāwiri, 'Whāngārei tribes', *Te Ara. The Encyclopedia of New Zealand,* updated 9 Nov 2012: http://www.TeAra.govt.nz/en/whangarei-tribes

Thomas, B.W., and R.H. Taylor, 'A history of ground-based rodent eradication techniques developed in New Zealand, 1859-1993', in Veitch and Clout, pp.301-310.

Towns, D.R., 'Eradications of invertebrate pests from islands around New Zealand. What have we delivered and what have we learned?', in Veitch, Clout and Towns, pp.364-371.

Tūroa, Taimoana, *Te Takoto o te Whenua o Hauraki. Hauraki landmarks*, (ed) Te Ahukaramū Charles Royal, Auckland, 2000.

Veitch, C.R. and M.N. Clout (eds), *Turning the Tide. The eradication of invasive species,* Proceedings of the International Conference on eradication of island invasives, Cambridge, 2002.

Veitch, C.R., M.N. Clout and D.R. Towns (eds), *Island Invasives. Eradications and Management,* Auckland, 2011.

Veitch, C.R., 'The eradication of feral cats (*Felis catus*) from Little Barrier Island, New Zealand', *New Zealand Journal of Zoology*, 28:1, 2001, pp.1-12.

Veitch, C.R. 'Eradication of Norway rats (*Rattus norvegicus*) and house mouse (*Mus musculus*) from Browns Island (Motukorea), Hauraki Gulf, New Zealand, in Veitch and Clout, pp.350-356.

Veitch, C.R., 'Eradication of Pacific rats (*Rattus exulans*) from Fanal Island, New Zealand, in Veitch and Clout, pp.357-359.

Veitch, C.R., 'Eradication of Pacific rats (*Rattus exulans*) from Tiritiri Matangi island, Hauraki Gulf, New Zealand', in Veitch and Clout, pp.360-364.

Waitangi Tribunal: http://www.justice.govt.nz/tribunals/waitangi-tribunal

Waitangi Tribunal, *The Hauraki Report*, Wai 686, Wellington, 2006.

Wilson, E. Wilson, 'Kawau – Island of Dreams. Memories of Sir George Grey', *The New Zealand Railways Magazine*, 2 December 1935, pp.33-38.

Woodley, Keith, *Godwits. Long-haul champions*, Auckland, 2009.

Wray, J. W., *South Sea Vagabonds*, Auckland, 1939.

Wright, Olive, *New Zealand 1826-1827 from the French of Dumont D'Urville*, Wellington, 1950.

Index